B®ANDLife

First published and distributed by
viction:workshop ltd.

## viction:ary™

viction:workshop ltd.
Unit C, 7/F, Seabright Plaza, 9-23 Shell Street,
North Point, Hong Kong
Url: www.victionary.com
Email: we@victionary.com
@victionworkshop
@victionary_
@victionworkshop

Edited and produced by viction:ary

Concept & art direction by Victor Cheung
Book design by viction:workshop ltd.

©2020 viction:workshop ltd.
All rights reserved. No part of this publication
may be reproduced, stored in retrieval systems,
or transmitted in any form or by any electronic
or mechanical means, including but not limited
to photocopying, recording, or any information
storage methods, without written permission from
the respective copyright owners.

All copyrights on text and design work are held
by the respective designers and contributors.
All artwork and textual information in this book
are based on the materials offered by the
designers whose work has been included. While
every effort has been made to ensure their
accuracy, viction:workshop does not accept any
responsibility, under any circumstances, for any
errors or omissions.

ISBN 978-988-79033-9-0
Printed and bound in China

RAW by WEIJENBERG

B®ANDLife

# Restaurants & Bars
Integrated brand systems in graphics and space

# BUCK.STUDIO

Dominika Buck, Founder & Head Designer

When our studio decided to specialise in hospitality and retail design 10 years ago, all we knew was that one could only became good at something that one really liked. We, for instance, loved great food and travels, so we owe our career path choice to our personal passions and interests more than anything else. After all, what could be more pleasant and exciting than researching restaurants and bars while travelling, tasting food, meeting passionate clients and talented chefs, learning how they work, and creating spaces that were meant to make people satiated and happy?

In those early days, we believed (and still do) that a project would only be good if we had strong faith in it and worked on it as if it was for ourselves. We also liked to imagine the fun we eventually would have just by spending time enjoying the places we designed, while having great meals and drinking wine with our satisfied clients.

Thankfully, all this has actually come true, as the result of our constant quest for knowledge and creativity as well as some serious responsibilities, really hard work, some sleepless nights and a couple of panic attacks during site visits! Along the way, we managed to get our projects published, receive a few design awards, and gain some rather unexpected international recognition that eventually led us to being asked to write the foreword for this book which is just as surprising and rewarding.

Our studio is based in Poland, where the F&B market is relatively young and rapidly developing. Most of the gastronomic ventures here were started by passionate individuals rather than hospitality specialists, and although clients are becoming more aware that a great restaurant is much more than a good-looking interior, most of their knowledge and experiences of running a successful F&B brand are still being gleaned from international standards.

Therefore, in our opinion, one of the biggest challenges today for designers like ourselves – not only here in Poland but globally as well – is creating an F&B business that is most of all authentic, with a unique concept related to or inspired by local context rather than global patterns and trends.

Behind every great F&B project is not excellent interior design alone, but a brilliant concept as well. A unique idea that defines and distinguishes the brand and the place; fusing all the elements of its identity and strategy including culinary profile, customer group, service standards, marketing communications, as well as branding and interior design. We strongly believe that a great concept makes the basis of great design, and in turn, consistency in executing it makes the place itself successful.

Although a well-executed concept helps to create an engaging atmosphere and unique customer experience, we have learned over time that in terms of design, the most important decisions are not about making things the boldest, most vivid, colourful or flashy, but the ones that actually make a difference. We always keep in mind that originality and uniqueness start where comparisons end.

This is why we let the bespoke details tell the story in all our designs. Whether it is through furniture and lighting pieces or accessories, our discerning approach builds up a brand's genuineness, personality, and unique style. And as the featured projects in this book also demonstrate, style is something that lasts when fashion and trends pass.

Ultimately, it is all about creating something meaningful and truly timeless.

"We always keep in mind that originality and uniqueness start when comparisons end."

"Only by being granted creative freedom can we push ourselves further and bring our output to the next level."

# Thinking*Room

Eric Widjaja, Design Principal

Since 2005, Thinking*Room has been striving to make things that matter, and with viction:ary having a similar mission within the publishing industry, I am glad that our paths have converged in the form of a foreword for this exciting new edition of BRANDLife.

As a comprehensive branding and graphic design company, our studio work continues to span across multiple mediums with ideas that go beyond mere 'labels'. After a modest start all those years ago, we have since gained a lot more experience in developing branding identities for food and beverage (F&B) companies as well as their various touch-points; having collaborated with several high-profile F&B brands to date such as Union, Biko and Sarirasa Group. We are excited to see our capabilities and portfolio keep on growing along with our clients' trust; a sense of camaraderie that has always been important to us, as it has enabled us to explore new concepts and directions. Only by being granted creative freedom can we push ourselves further and bring our output to the next level.

In our F&B journey, many lessons were learnt along the way, but if I have to single out the most important one, it would have to be to know 'good' clients. Equipped with razor-sharp vision, 'good' clients can articulate what they really want, which we can then translate into a compelling brand direction. We can also help them to 'score' goals, as the latter would be clearly defined. After all, you cannot score a goal if you don't know where the goal posts are! Personally, I also think that it is essential to collaborate closely with professionals in other fields, such as interior designers, food consultants, and contractors, because their perspectives and different skill-sets can complement ours.

Looking at the bigger picture, the contemporary dining and drinking scene in Jakarta is growing rapidly today. Many F&B brands have started to bloom, and I certainly hope that the industry will continue to flourish because of the resulting benefits to the economy and the people. With new options popping up in terms of cuisines and customer experiences, it is fulfilling to me that job seekers are finding new opportunities. As this has also led to increasing competition, the need to stand out is more important than ever before – not just in terms of product quality (which has to be good, obviously), but also in branding – and this is where our expertise comes in.

As much as craft is important, I believe that being inspired to grow and evolve is key to being a good designer. This book makes the perfect starting point for aspiring creatives and those seeking out new ideas; and I hope that your mind becomes more open to new creative possibilities by learning from the successful projects within.

# Contents

Food and beverage (F&B) are more than just sources of nourishment to be consumed and forgotten. Since time immemorial, they have held the power to unite people across all ages, cultures, and identities, in that the simple act of enjoying meals or drinks together – even amongst strangers – can form the basis for memories and relationships that last a lifetime. To facilitate these connections, the best restaurants and bars today know how important it is to offer remarkable culinary experiences amidst thoughtfully designed environments. On top of setting the right atmosphere for customers via compelling interiors and architecture, creative concepts and cuisines can be brought to life and complemented by cohesive visual identities for truly immersive multisensorial encounters.

## Index of abbreviations

| | |
|------|------------------------|
| **AD** | Art direction |
| **AR** | Architecture |
| **CD** | Creative direction |
| **CL** | Client(s) |
| **FD** | Food design |
| **ID** | Graphic identity / design |
| **IN** | Interior design |
| **LT** | Lighting |
| **PH** | Photography |
| **SC** | Special credit(s) |

# NoHo
# HOSPITALITY

Michelin-starred establishments aside, New York City is fast becoming a mecca for lovers of innovative food and beverage concepts. Often hailed as the land of opportunity where dreams come to life, it has held no limits for the discerning and the daring who set up shop and strive for success; resulting in an increasingly robust culinary landscape that continues to expand and excite the epi-curious. Not many restaurants or bars manage to swim against the relentless tide of passing trends and stiff competition, but those that do possess the ingenuity, talent, and hunger to succeed—like NoHo Hospitality Group.

NoHo Hospitality is no stranger to experimentation. Armed with an assorted portfolio of restaurants and bars rooted in quality, character, culture, and culinary excellence, co-founders Chef Andrew Carmellini, Luke Ostrom, and Josh Pickard have been combining their strengths and skills to design dynamic and memorable dining experiences for the modern gourmand since 2009. Based in New York City where passion and perseverance are known to blur the line between success and survival, their concepts continue to stand out and stand firm to this day, as they balance innovation and timelessness to seduce, sate, and delight new and loyal patrons with their creativity and craft.
Photos: Noah Fecks

The best food and beverage (F&B) scenes around the world today boast an interesting amalgamation of culinary genius and creative concepts; where one can expect a confluence of influences that transcend backgrounds and boundaries. Along with the proliferation of the Internet and technological progress, the industry continues to evolve as a whole to accommodate the ever-changing needs of the capricious modern customer. Five-star ratings, reviews, and recommendations aside, what makes a restaurant or bar genuinely 'good' or special no longer depends on its menu or service alone. Rather, it takes a concerted effort through which compelling visuals and stories are interwoven into flavour to create a cohesive setting that offers feasts for the senses.

Although it was not considered to be a distinct dining destination in the past, New York City has slowly but surely drawn from its sizeable melting pot of contexts and cultures to emerge as a thriving hotspot for local and international foodies. Beyond the typical Michelin-starred, white-tablecloth establishments, a host of noteworthy eateries and watering holes have popped up in recent years; gaining their renown by demonstrating an acute understanding of present-day patrons through ideation, gumption, and taste.

02

01

01_Rye Street Tavern offers the perfect ambience for 'modern soul food' dining along
the Baltimore waterfront. Photo: Noah Fecks
02_Rustic farmhouse vibes and weathered
Eastern shore elements greet patrons at Rye
Street Tavern. Photo: Noah Fecks
03_The Library at The Public Theatre is one
of New York City's best-kept hidden gems.
Photo: Noah Fecks

03

# NOHO AND THE KNOW-HOW
# TO MAKE IT

NoHo Hospitality Group owns a range of restaurants and bars that are
bound together by this ability to resonate with a discerning, cosmopolitan
crowd. At the heart of its operations lies a dedication to excellence coupled
with a love for ideas; resulting in a diverse yet solid portfolio that includes
an American restaurant, bar, and oyster room; an Italian taverna inside
Robert DeNiro's TriBeCa hotel; a hallmark French grand café and bakery;
one of Rolling Stone magazine's top ten clubs in the USA; a casual pasta
shop; a seasonal restaurant; as well as a 22nd-floor rooftop bar.

Co-helmed by Luke Ostrom, Josh Pickard, and the award-winning Chef
Andrew Carmellini, NoHo Hospitality Group operates on the basis that
there is more to dining out than the 'Dish of the Day'. Design and details
are crucial in fusing form and function to bring the founders' innovative
ideas and collective vision to life. By providing people with the perfect
ambience and avenue to enjoy each other's company, their focus in
nourishing both the body and soul aptly demonstrates the meaning and
underlying purpose behind their brand name. In the following interview,
Luke (LO) and Chef Andrew (CA) reveal their secret recipes for success.

"The restaurants that we create offer guests more than a singular reason to come by and pay a visit. We put the same amount of focus on a solo diner at a table or the bar as much as we do on a large group."

04

05

06

04_Artist Eric Junker's lively murals adorn the walls of Lafayette in Manhattan. Photo: Noah Fecks
05_Chef Andrew Carmellini fuses fresh ingredients with creativity at The Dutch, NYC. Photo: Noah Fecks
06_Scrumptious tomahawk steak awaits at American landmark, Rec Pier Chop House. Photo: Noah Fecks
07_A cosy, casual-chic backdrop pairs well with the authentic Italian menu at San Morello. Photo: Shinola

07

### How did NoHo Hospitality Group come to be?

LO: Chef Carmellini and I have been working together for the last 18 years in New York, so there's a lot of history there! We had also known Josh for quite some time and looked at a couple of potential projects together before finally collaborating on the opening of Locanda Verde a decade ago. That was the beginning of NoHo Hospitality Group as we know it.

### Based on experience, what do you think are the factors necessary in creating a successful dining/drinking space?

LO: Wow, (they make) a really long list! It's the hundreds of details that you can see, and often, just as many that you don't see but can feel. We try to create a holistic experience for our guests. The visual identity is important, as are the lighting, the soundtrack, as well as the warm smiles and sincere hospitality from the team members who welcome our guests into our 'home'. Although food and drink are the main drivers of what people remember, now more than ever, interior design plays such an important role. Diners today are often looking for visual stimulation, whether it's on the plate, within their surroundings, or even the collateral that they are touching or bringing home with them.

### In coming together to make creative decisions, how do the each of you stay true to your own voices?

LO: My creative decision-making is often born out of a simple idea, or inspiration that I find throughout my day-to-day or during my travels. We always have a long running list of ideas. A menu often takes shape after we build a base narrative of the type of experience we are trying to create in a restaurant. We then try to create spaces that we would want to dine and hang out in ourselves.

### How does NoHo Hospitality Group set itself apart from the rest of its peers? What would you say are the distinct touches that make a restaurant or bar uniquely yours?

LO: The restaurants that we create offer guests more than a singular reason to come by and pay a visit. We put the same amount of focus on a solo diner at a table or the bar as much as we do on a large group. Compartmentalising a restaurant has been a strategy we use to create multiple intimate spaces as opposed to a vast open room. Lighting and sound always set the mood – we tend to have a ton of individual lights with specialised dimming controls to create that all-important glow that people look best in. There is also perhaps nothing more important than sound-proofing. Diners won't come back to a space that is unbearably loud, no matter how good the food and drink can be.

### So many factors go into a single project! How does the creative process usually unfold in the studio?

LO: We often look at ourselves as 'producers' with the intention of building a great stage for talented players to put on a great nightly show. As in any production, it often stems from a singular vision. Creatively nurturing that vision into a reality is not always easy, but it's how our restaurants come to life. We bring on good partners in architecture, interior design, and lighting; then assemble our internal team of talented specialists in development, service, cuisine, beverages, etc. It is important for us to keep each new restaurant a collaborative process. We have found that this is what gives us the best results.

08

### How do you ensure consistency in quality at every stage?

LO: Details, details, details! That said, it's certainly not easy. In such a human business, there is always a lot of room for error. Paying extra attention to all the details and having a big team working together by keeping their eye out for each other helps. We have learned a lot over the years, both the good and the bad.

### With all the learnings so far, you have built quite an excellent reputation. Are you typically under a lot of pressure to consistently deliver and surprise patrons?

CA: We have been fortunate to share the pressure of product delivery and surprise at our restaurants by building new concepts around an extremely talented group of team members who give each one a refreshing sense of individuality personality-wise. In many cases, our veteran team members have become our partners, and their frontline ownership spreads the pressure of delivering quality product and hospitality in a generally tough business with so many variables to control day-to-day.

### What values do you look for in your team members?

CA: We look for team members who smile, are tenacious, energetic, consistent, and lead by example. We hope to find individuals who are optimistic and positive thinkers; ones who would never say 'no' to guest requests. The delivery of consistency in F&B and hospitality is mostly based upon managing and controlling the details of limitless repetitive and defined tasks. It takes people who are not afraid to tackle the hard tasks each and every day to build success.

### For those unfamiliar with the F&B scene in NYC, how has it evolved over the last 10 years?

CA: In NYC, it certainly has become relatively more expensive than when I started out in 1990 with Time Café (now called Lafayette). Every aspect of developing restaurants is more difficult today. Record-pace rising real estate costs, construction, permitting requirements, and labour costs have made it almost impossible to start out unless you have access to considerable capital. However, we are beginning to see signs of declining prices in retail leases pushed by a noticeable level of vacancies across the city and many big cities globally. There are far more landlords today who are interested in deals with restaurant operators – who until recently were pushed out by large brand retailers who were less concerned about leasing costs and happy to create a loss-leading marketing vehicle to push brand awareness.

### Do trends ever influence what you do?

CA: We tend to focus less on trends when designing the physical spaces of new concepts. Open kitchen design and display cooking became a trend at one point, I assume, and we continue to incorporate it into every restaurant we build. More than ever today, certainly after 26 years of Food Network, people love to watch chefs demonstrate their craft. We do believe that 26 years of food television has educated the dining public globally, which has created a new demand for culinary-focused food in the quick-service dining market. We are therefore developing some concepts that are more quick-service oriented but also stay true to our culinary and hospitality discipline.

### Besides coming up with new concepts, what is the near-future looking like for NoHo Hospitality Group?

LO: We have been really fulfilled by the growth path that we have been on over the last few years, which has resulted in about one new project a year. We hope to pursue more opportunities in markets that are new to us outside of New York, like our recent openings in Baltimore and Detroit.

09

10

11

# Graphic Identities

Visualising brands in print

Many factors play a part when it comes to choosing a venue for dining out or indulging in a tipple, with overall standards, preferences, and levels of comfort being the most persuasive. Although people rarely give graphic identities of restaurants and bars a second look, there is more to them than meets the eye. Whether it is setting the tone for the experience to come before one steps into the establishment or strengthening the concept of the food or drinks being served, the following projects demonstrate the power that they have to attract and resonate with patrons by embodying an outlet's personality in eye-catching ways.

# COMETA

San Pedro Garza García, Mexico

COMETA is a gastro-bar in downtown San Pedro Garza García offering culinary creations by one of Mexico's best chefs. Chapter were inspired by the country's north-eastern gastronomic culture and the Art Deco movement to create a dynamic visual identity that merged traditional and modern values. Focusing on an eye-catching and layered typographic system, they set out to complement the establishment's fun and relaxed atmosphere with clean lines, pronounced angles, and a unique pattern incorporating classic Mexican elements – resulting in a cohesive and compelling branding suite that matches the memorable dining experience.

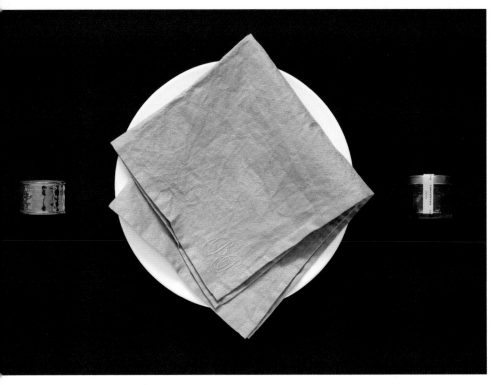

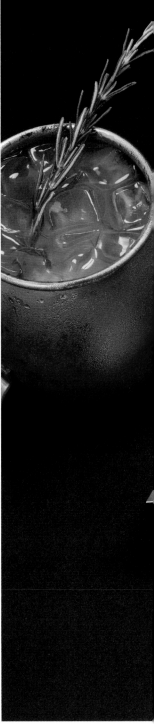

# Bistrot Pasquinel

Puebla, Mexico

**ID** Anagrama    **CL** Bistrot Pasquinel

Besides serving up a unique world of fresh and refined flavours, Bistrot Pasquinel in Puebla also provides patrons with interactive dining experiences that fuse the dynamism of its open kitchen with the intimacy of its cosy lounge and terrace. In designing a cohesive visual identity for the restaurant, Anagrama created an intriguing blend of the region's inherent spirit of hospitality and their own contemporary interpretation of elegance to set the tone for memorable culinary encounters. The juxtapositon of typefaces, foiled accents on muted colours, and vintage illustrations also serve to allude to a sense of subtle luxury.

BISTROT
**PASQUINEL**

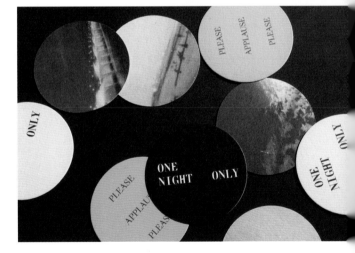

# One Night Only

Singapore, Singapore

**ID & IN** Foreign Policy Design Group     **CL** One Night Only

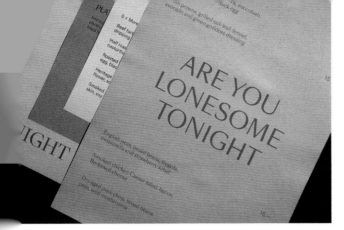

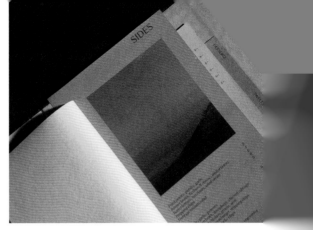

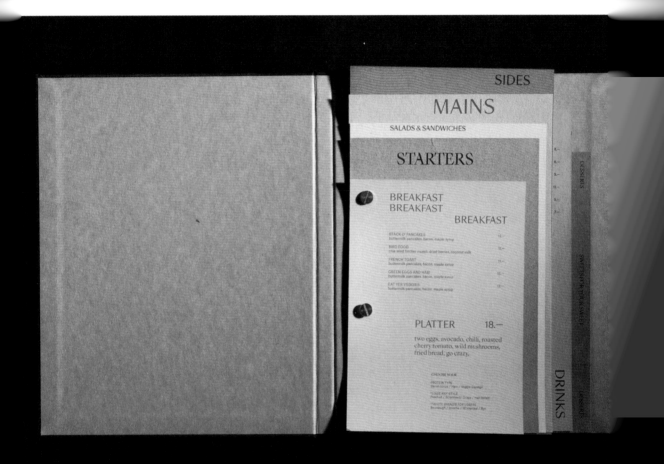

Foreign Policy Design Group's branding and interior work for One Night Only captures the spirit of youthful irreverence, adventure, and carefree romanticism that all-American road trips stand for. In referencing the time-honoured quest for the best food across the country, its printed materials feature abstract landscape imagery peppered with typefaces reminiscent of old noir films and intimate handwritten script evoking the fleeting sense of melancholy that long drives sometimes entail. Brass fittings complement the space's primary colour palette of green and blue with wood and marble surfaces to present a modern and chic interpretation of the classic diner experience.

# Hokkaidon

Hong Kong, Hong Kong

**ID** A Work of Substance    **PH** Vita Mak    **CL** 1957 & co. Restaurant Group

For Hokkaidon's visual identity, A Work of Substance set out to 'disrupt' the tranquility of the traditional 'seigaiha' or blue sea wave motif in a refreshing and aesthetically appealing way. Around the restaurant, an array of aquatic life can be seen 'breaking through' uniformed ocean lines on the patterned wall murals – reflecting the renewed vigour with which it endeavours to bring Japanese heritage and values to life. Its logo is inspired and characterised by grains of rice, the humble foundation of Japanese cuisine and culture, to strike a balance between the palpable energy of its modern sea-to-table offerings and the pure authenticity that emanates from the essence of 'chirashi'.

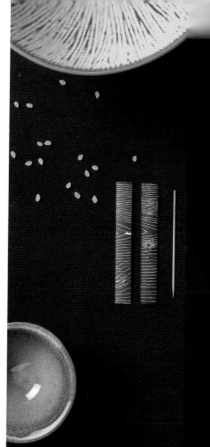

# Lok Hue Hng

Taipei, Taiwan

**ID** HOUTH    **IN** ANYROOM STUDIO    **CL** Lok Hue Hng

Located in the diverse, cosmopolitan city of Taipei, Lok Hue Hng strives to create a contemporary dining experience using traditional Taiwanese elements. Besides infusing classic Taiwanese herbs into its specialty cocktails, the bar and cafe features live local folk music performances on weekends to attract the young and young-at-heart. To reflect its compelling mix of old-meets-new, HOUTH used classic patterned grilles and glass windows as the inspiration for its logo design. They subsequently combined these elements with the symmetry typically found in Chinese paper-cutting and Western-influenced linework to define a unique style brimming with character.

# Plum & Spilt Milk

London, United Kingdom

**ID** Here Design     **PH** Eddie Jacobs     **CL** Plum & Spilt Milk

For Plum & Spilt Milk, a modern restaurant within the Great Northern Hotel in London serving beautifully cooked British classics, Here Design were inspired by their discovery that the livery colours used on the first-ever Great Northern Railway dining carriage were maroon and cream, also known as plum and spilt milk. Besides creating a visual identity that heroes its name, they also paid homage to plum fruit in a playful way. Overall, its brand collateral seamlessly complement the interiors, for which glasses, silverware, and centrepiece items were specially sourced to bring its unique concept to life.

## PLUM + SPILT MILK

### STARTERS

Potted shrimp Rocket, melba toast **6**

Haddock soufflé Quails egg, herring roe cream **7**

Gruyere crouton **5**

soda bread **6**

Terrine Ham hock, foie gras, prunes **7.5**

breads Red wine sauce, root vegetables **7.5**

### MAINS

Day **12**

tomato **16**

de **18**

Hollandaise **3**

utney, cider sauce **16**

adder Parsnip mash **16**

les, glazed potatoes **13.5**

# Tonchin

New York, USA

ID LMNOP    IN Carpenter + Mason    PH Nicole Franzen (Interior & Food)
SC Helen Levi (Ceramic Lamps), Salt + Still (Noren)    CL Tonchin New York

For the USA debut of Tonchin, the acclaimed chain of ramen-focused restaurants originating in Tokyo, LMNOP created a unique visual identity by giving traditional Japanese design an unmistakably New York twist. The bold geometric patterns found around the restaurant such as the menus, custom-made crockery, and servers' scarves, not only formed endless combinations much like a bowl of ramen itself, but also served as a nice contrast to its organic textures. Besides working closely with the interior designers, the studio also commissioned textile artist Alison Charli to transform their patterns into a hand-stitched noren to honour Japanese craftsmanship.

# Common Lot

New Jersey, USA

**ID** Perky Bros  **IN** Studio 1200  **PH** Daniel Krieger (Interior & Food), Brett Warren (Design)  **CL** Ehren Ryan

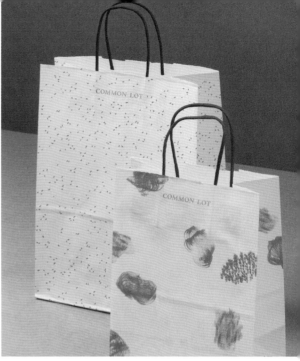

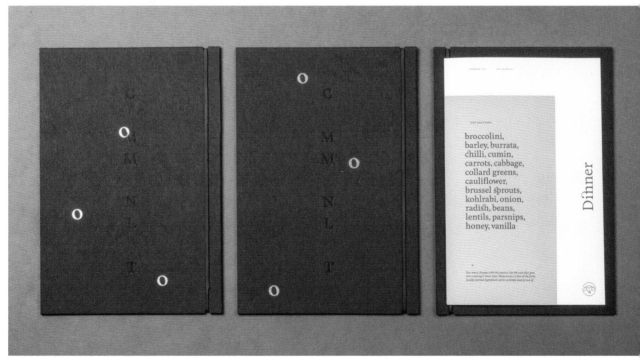

Common Lot drew upon Chef Ehren Ryan's globally diverse background and free spirit to focus on the communal dining experience with an open kitchen and shared tables. Inspired by this ethos and the owners' part-serious, part-jocular approach to cooking and life, Perky Bros were driven by the idea of a common pasture with wayward sheep and shared plates. By playfully moving the letter 'O's in the logotype and stamping abstract sheep illustrations on the brand collateral, the resulting work is unpredictable and at times rough around the edges, but always intentional and thoughtful – reflecting the stylish but unpretentious charm of the space and its hosts.

# Earls 67

Calgary, Canada

**ID** Glasfurd & Walker    **IN** Ste. Marie    **PH** Jaime Hyatt (Room), Eydis Einarsdóttir (Parrot)    **CL** Earls Restaurant

With 66 locations around Canada and the USA, Earls has been at the leading edge of customer care and dining culture for over 30 years. In recognising the need to keep on innovating, it commissioned Glasfurd & Walker to create a one-off protopye restaurant called Earls 67, where new food, service, and décor ideas could be developed and rolled out to the other outlets. Inspired by everything that made the brand what it is today, the studio revitalised its existing narrative by adding energy and elements of experimentation into its updated visual identity, giving it a more globalised and contemporary new look.

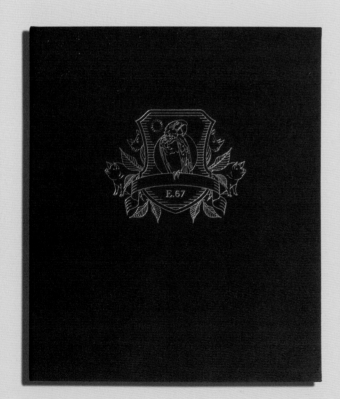

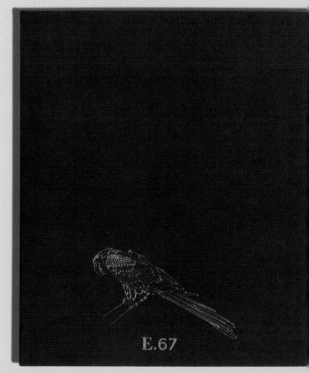

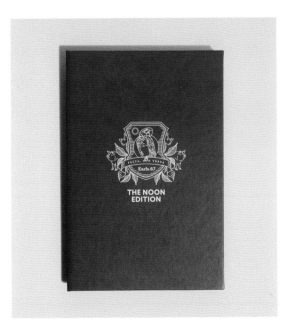

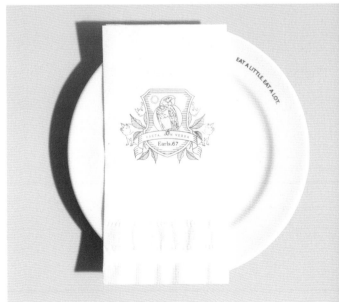

# Souk

Melbourne, Australia

**ID** Mildred & Duck    **PH** Shelley Horan    **CL** Souk

Vlad Kovacevic

0410 703 363
vlad@soukmelbourne.com.au

Souk

13 Bligh Place
Melbourne 3000

03 8597 5444
merhaba@soukmelbourne.com.au
soukmelbourne.com.au

Hidden down an alleyway off Flinder's Lane in Melbourne is a portal to the Middle East called Souk, a restaurant and bar that serves a modern take on the region's cuisine. Mildred & Duck's eye-popping branding suite playfully re-interprets the way Arabic is read from right to left – a fun visual device that features prominently throughout the space and has become a part of the entire dining experience. Besides bucking the trend of minimalism with an indulgent aesthetic reminiscent of vibrant, overfilled bazaars, they also created a memorable logomark by giving the traditional 'evil eye' a contemporary twist – resulting in an overall look-and-feel that is full of colour and character.

juice, grapn... Grape and rose
... garnished with pistachio                                    $17

MARTINI
... sugar and Turkish coffee                                    $21

tonic and watermelon spritz                          $15

... simple syrup, egg white                      $16

... grape molasses, rose                    $18
... x and amber              $19

**\*\*\*\*\*\*\*\*\*\*\*\*\*\*\*\*\*\*\*\*\*\*\*\*\*\*\*\*\*\*\*\*\*\* WINE \*\*\*\*\*\*\*\*\*\*\*\*\*\*\*\*\*\*\*\*\*\*\*\***

SPARKLING

| | | | |
|---|---|---|---|
| NV | Castellargo Brut DOC Prosecco | | |
| NV | Moores Hill Blanc de Blancs | Veneto, Italy | |
| NV | Boizel Brut Reserve | Tamar Valley, TAS | $10/46 |
| 2018 | Veuve Clicquot | Epernay, France | $70 |
| | Mister Fox Moscato | Champagne, France | $19.95 |
| | | Central Victoria | $140 |

WHITE

| | | | |
|---|---|---|---|
| 2015 | Penna Lane Watervale Riesling | | $9.5/45 |
| 2014 | Kallstadt Saumagen Riesling | Clare Valley, SA | |
| 2018 | Buckley's Sauvignon Blanc | Pfalz, Germany | $12/56 |
| 2018 | Eradus Sauvignon Blanc | Geelong, VIC | $45 |
| 2014 | Chateau Kefraya Blanc De Blancs | Marlborough, NZ | |
| 2016 | Victoria Avenue Pinot Grigio | Beqaa Valley, Lebanon | $41 |
| 2014 | Vinkara Doruk Narince | King Valley, VIC | $10/48 |
| 2015 | Suvla Kinali Yapincak | Tokat, Turkey | $48 |
| 2015 | Borgo Viscone Pinot Grigio | Gallipoli, Turkey | $42 |
| 2015 | Baddaginnie Run Verdelho | Friuli, Italy | $39 |
| 2013 | Sevilen Isabey Sauvignon Blanc | Strathbogie Ranges, VIC | $11/52 |
| 2013 | Badel Traminac Nespes | Izmir, Turkey | |
| 2015 | Nova Vita Firebird Chardonnay | Zelina, Croatia | $44 |
| 2012 | Moores Hill Chardonnay | Adelaide Hills, SA | $41 |
| 2015 | Charles Monserat Chablis | Tamar Valley, TAS | $36 |
| | Santo Wines Nykteri Assyrtiko | Burgundy, France | $13/60 |
| | | Santorini, Greece | $68 |
| | | | $79 |
| | | | $10/38 |

**\*\*\*\*\*\*\*\*\*\*\*\*\*\*\*\*\*\*\*\*\* SHARE \*\*\*\*\*\*\*\*\*\*\*\*\*\*\*\*\*\*\*\*\***

SHOOK-RUN
Pick any 4 items from the menu

THE TOSUN PAŞA!
Pick any 6 items from the menu                                  $45pp

YALLA HABIBI
Pick any 8 items from the menu
                                                               $55pp

Minimum two people, all table members need to take
part. All dietary requirements will be catered for
with notice upon request.                                      $65pp

))))))))))))))))))))) MEZE (((((((((((((((((((((

CHIPOTLE HUMMUS
Chickpeas and chipotle, drizzled with
burnt butter and paprika (GF) (V)                        $9

MIDYE DOLMA: STUFFED MUSSELS (4PC)
Mussels filled with fragrant rice, black
pepper and baharat spices, served at
room temperature (GF)                                    $14

BAMYA/BAMIEH: STEWED OKRA AND TOMATO
Okra cooked Yemeni-style, slowly
simmered in tomato, fresh chilli,
coriander, and red papri...
served with fried si...

KISIR

OOOOOOOOOOOOOOOO MEZE

RAKI MEZE
Haloumi, watermelon, marin...
pickled vegetables, chipot...
walnuts and tomato dip serv...
tomato jam (GF) (V)

SOFT SHELL CRAB PITTA POCKET
Za'taar and dukkah-spiced soft-...
crab with Lebanese red cabbage w...
(GF option)

CHARCOAL OCTOPUS
Octopus with hot muhammara sauce,
roasted potato and herb oil (GF)

SHAWARMA: ARABIAN TACOS (4pc, 1 of each)
Slow-cooked lamb with cucumber, red
radish, mixed leaves, cherry to...
and spring onion with a ho...
coriander mayonnaise.
Grilled chicken...
radish, mi...
and sp...

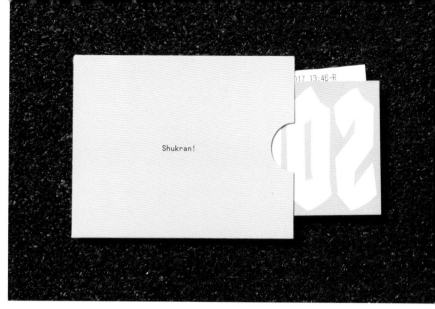

Shukran!

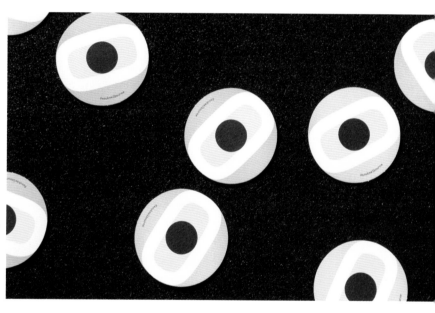

# Meissl & Schadn – Schnitzel Love

Vienna, Austria

**ID** moodley brand identity   **IN** Florian Weitzer   **CL** Weitzer Hotels BetriebsgesmbH

The legendary Meissl & Schadn stands for everything that once made Viennese cuisine famous, and continues to be a luminary in the local and international dining scene. To translate the culinary leaders' visual language from the past into the present, moodley brand identity were inspired by the concept of old-meets-new, combining classic elements with unconventional ones to create a memorable branding suite that bridged decades. Besides applying a timeless pink and gold colour combination, they also retained the use of Romana, the original typeface used in the restaurant's menus at the turn of the century, as a homage to the Austrian's undying love for schnitzel.

Kaiju Dining Sdn. Bhd.

Kaiju. Thai Style Ryōri.
Lot S4, APW Bangsar.
29 Jalan Riong,
59100 Kuala Lumpur.
+603 2788 3796
FB. IG. KaijuCompany

# Kaiju Company

Kuala Lumpur, Malaysia

**ID** LIE DESIGN & ART DIRECTION    **IN** POW Ideas    **SP** Driv Loo (Art Direction & Design)    **CL** Kaiju Company

As the first Japanese-Thai fusion restaurant in Kuala Lumpur, Kaiju needed to set the right tone and mood through their branding and interior design. Inspired by the word 'kaiju' itself, which refers to a Japanese film genre featuring giant monsters, LIE created an eye-catching visual identity revolving around Godzilla, the renowned prehistoric beast from the 1970s movie, and an intimidating Thai Dragon as its formidable opponent and nemesis. During the creative process, they also worked closely with the interior designer to infuse a rich blend of Japanese and Thai influences into a cohesive aesthetic that reflects the one-of-a-kind dining experience that patrons can expect.

Opening Hours...

Thai Style
Ryori

Lot 5C, 5FW Banquet
25 Jalan Riong,
59100 Kuala Lumpur.
+603 2788 3796
FB/IG: KaijuCompany

kaiju

#KaijuCompany

# Rey's Place

Sydney, Australia

**ID** Re    **PH** Nick Lawrence    **SC** Rey's Place (Food Design)    **CL** Rey's Place

Re found a way to bridge the culinary divide in designing the visual language for Rey's Place, the first Filipino fine-dining restaurant in Sydney. Located within a heritage-listed terrace house with two levels that offer distinct experiences, it offers patrons the option to 'sip and savour' within a sublime and refined setting on the top floor; or 'drink and devour' amid the cool and stripped-back atmosphere of the shot-smashing bar below. Across offline and online platforms, the brand identity represents both characteristics of the venue through two custom typefaces based on Filipino calligraphy, a two-tone colour palette, as well as the use of contrasting imagery.

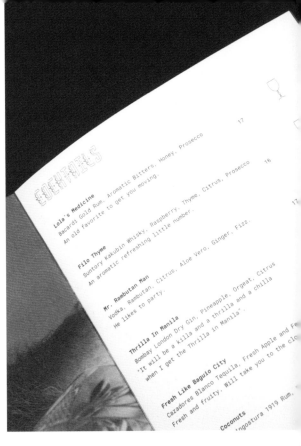

## COCKTAILS

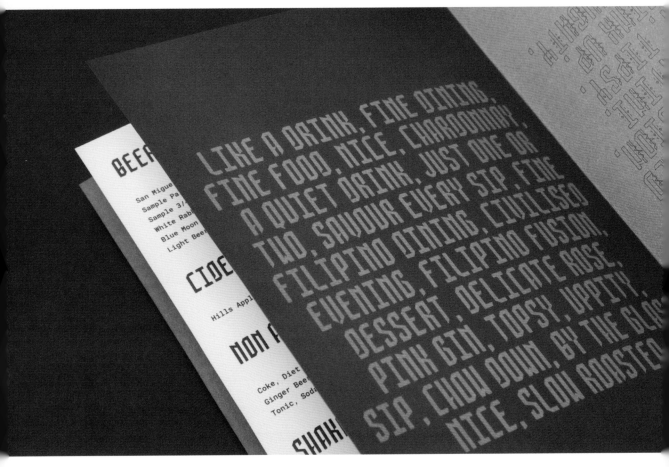

LIKE A DRINK, FINE DINING, FINE FOOD, NICE, CHARDONNAY, A QUIET DRINK, JUST ONE OR TWO, SAVOUR EVERY SIP, FINE FILIPINO DINING, CIVILISED EVENING, FILIPINO FUSION, DESSERT, DELICATE ROSE, PINK GIN, TOPSY, UPPITY, SIP, CHOW DOWN, BY THE GLOS, NICE, SLOW ROASTED

### BEER
San Migue
Sample Pa
Sample 3/
White Rab
Blue Moon
Light Beer

### CIDE
Hills Appl

### NON A
Coke, Diet
Ginger Bee
Tonic, Soda

### SHAK

Chicke...
Sweet soy glazed ...
Beef fillet, smoked chilli

**MAKI** マキ

ar,
.17
moked eggplant

California, fresh crab mayo,
spring onion, avocado, tobiko ........... 7.

Spider, softshell crab, wasabi mayo,
shredded cabbage, cucumber ........... 7.6

zu ........... 14.5

Dynamite ebi tempura ...........

ng salmon,
........... 18.9

Tiger prawns tempura, kimchi, burd...
tuna & truffle, tuna belly, ponzu, tr...

ed sea bream, ponzu
........... 15

Salmon & avocado, cucumber ...........

Chirashi salad, mixed fresh sea...
ponzu & shredded lettuce

Vegetable & salad, fresh ve...
light wafu ........... 5

Please inform your waiter of any allergy or dietary
requirements when making your order.
Prices include VAT at 20%.
10% discretionary charge will be added to your bill.

# Issho

Leeds, United Kingdom

**ID** Dutchscot    **CL** D&D London

Okinawa Cinn...
Yuzu Curd, Chocolate...

Warm Rice Pudding, Caramelised B...

Special Chocolate & Matcha Pudding

Chef's selection dessert platter,
served with sorbets & ice creams (serves 3)                    22,5

7

tuce,

For Issho, a word that translates to 'together' in Japanese, the idea of togetherness permeates the restaurant's visual identity. Besides subtly manifesting it in their design work through the double 's' glyph logo within the 'hanko' seal, Dutchscot cohesively applied the concept of 'kintsugi' across all branding collateral, as seen in the single-minded use of the copper join on printed materials like the food and drink menus, to add more meaning to the aesthetics. They also created a British pattern, a Japanese pattern, and a combined pattern with London-based pattern house, Eley Kishimoto, to strengthen the core idea.

一緒

**ISSHO**
Victoria Gate, Leeds LS2 7AU
+44 (0)113 426 5000
info@issho-restaurant.com
@isshoLDS

DRINK

# Bambudda

Vancouver, Canada

**ID** Post Projects    **IN** Ste. Marie    **PH** Jennilee Marigomen, Grady Mitchell    **CL** Bambudda

Serving a delicious mix of modern Hong Kong and southern Chinese cuisine, Bambudda was a contemporary Chinese restaurant located in Vancouver's historic Gastown district. In revitalising its visual identity to resonate well with the interior space, Post Projects breathed new life into the existing Timonium typeface – giving its jazz associations and retrospective influences a modern twist. Overall, the classic furniture complemented the colour palette and high-quality combination of materials, bamboo textures, and gold foiled accents to exude more character and charm.

# BAMBUDDA
99 POWELL STREET
5:30 - MIDNIGHT, TUESDAY-SUNDAY
CLOSED MONDAYS

# ORANGE

Fuzhou, China

**ID** Ideando    **IN** Xiang Gao, Juzi    **CL** ORANGE Bar

Although the colour in ORANGE's namesake had to feature prominently throughout the cocktail lounge's visual identity, Ideando set out to push their level of creativity further. Complementing the bilingual typography and stamp effect in its simple yet striking logo is the geometric visual element that is reminiscent of a halved orange fruit. Throughout the space, the logotype is embossed or carved onto different materials like leather and wood for customised items like lighter holders, coasters, and badges for added texture. The wall feature, a darkly humorous quote in bright neon, adds a rebellious touch to the sense of modern sophistication in the venue.

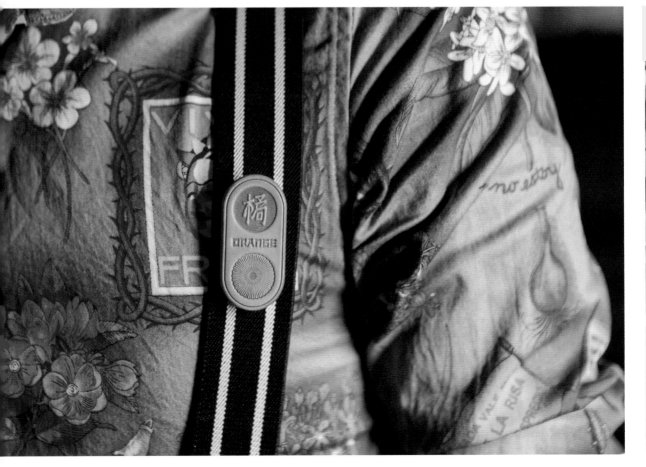

# bunker

Ho Chi Minh City, Vietnam

**ID** The Lab Saigon    **CL** bunker

An homage to good vibes, bunker is a unique bed-and-breakfast venue with a bar in Ho Chi Minh City. A venture by The Lab Saigon, its concept was inspired by the real, irreverent, and run-down neighbourhood haunts of Los Angeles's Chinatown in the early 1990s. In translating the era's authentic and gritty street vibes to the space, the studio sought to 'capture the prevailing mood of the period – not of Pinterest'. Rather than focus on perfection, they looked to convey their moody interpretations of a specific time and place in a 'real' and stylish manner using unpretentious type, colour, and design schemes.

# Pippo

Jakarta, Indonesia

**ID** Thinking*Room  **CL** Biko Group

An upper middle-class Italian cafe based in Jakarta, Pippo serves classic dishes like pizzas and pastas to those who crave authentic and delicious Italian delicacies. In creating its visual identity, Thinking*Room were mindful of keeping their work simple and warm. Besides deriving its logo design from a child looking longingly at a tomato, an iconic ingredient, they also applied the fruit's red tone with touches of green to represent the fresh vegetables that are prominent in the cuisine. To bring the entire look together, yellow was used to complement the two hues and reflect the venue's welcoming vibes.

# Kanpai!

Jakarta, Indonesia

**ID** Thinking*Room  **CL** Hiro Group

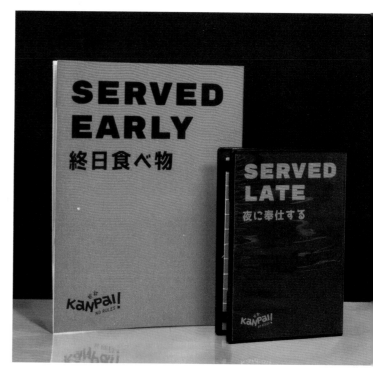

Kanpai, or 'cheers' in Japanese, is a themed bar in an upscale part of Northern Jakarta that embraces the philosophy where people are more prone to opening up and being their honest selves when inebriated. Based on this way of thinking, as well as a Japanese phenomenon called 'nomu-nication' where 'nomu'

means 'to drink', Thinking*Room were inspired to select a tanuki as the mascot for the bar's visual identity. In Japanese folklore, the creature is said to have a mischievous nature that compels it to shape-shift and trick people, but it cannot maintain its disguises when drunk – literally causing it to reveal its true self.

# LIONIMAGINE

Fuzhou, China

**ID** Ideando   **IN** Ruo Shan Chen She Interior   **CL** LIONIMAGINE

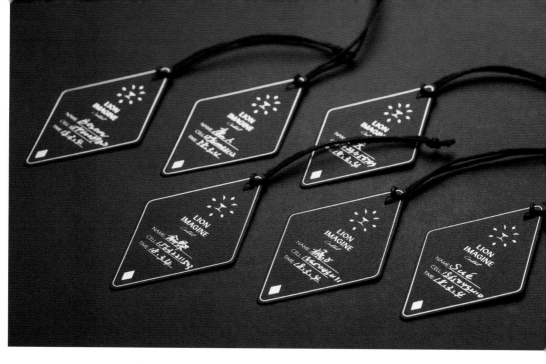

In designing LIONIMAGINE's visual identity, Ideando were inspired by the fact that 'drinking requires a sense of ritualism', where the atmosphere needs to be conducive for true appreciation. The logo is a clever representation of the king of the jungle, using a cocktail glass surrounded by diamond shapes in golden foil on black – the latter combination being the core colour palette across brand collateral. To reflect the owner's deep interest in movies, the wide variety of wines offered by the bar were named after famous flicks like The Lion King and One Day.

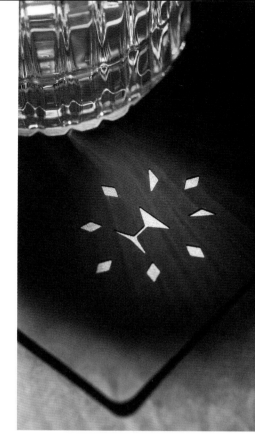

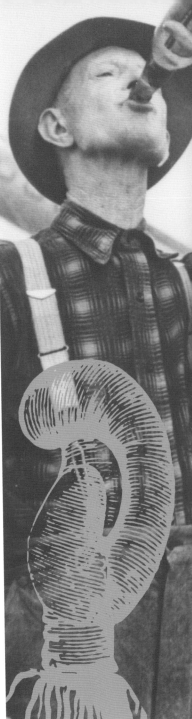

# Haymaker

Charlotte, USA

**ID & IL** SDCO Partners      **IN** Square Feet Studios      **PH** Peter Frank Edwards      **CL** William Dissen

Haymaker Restaurant brings locally inspired, seasonal food by Chef Wiliam Dissen to the Queen City. Using the two definitions of its namesake, a person who is involved in the making of hay and a forceful blow, SDCO Partners designed a visual identity featuring an eclectic mix of farming and boxing imagery, as well as custom illustrations. While the menus are presented in a simple manner, multiple papers and layouts create balance in the way that they offer moments of surprise and delight. Thoughtful branded touchpoints such as drink stirrers, coasters, and to-go bags were also customised for a cohesive dining experience.

Make Hay
While the Sun
Shines.

CLT · NC 28202

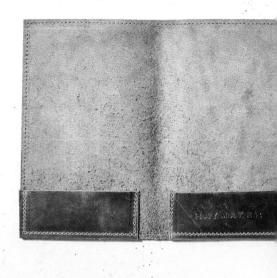

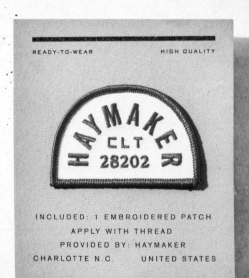

READY-TO-WEAR                    HIGH QUALITY

HAYMAKER
CLT
28202

INCLUDED: 1 EMBROIDERED PATCH

APPLY WITH THREAD

PROVIDED BY: HAYMAKER

CHARLOTTE N.C.          UNITED STATES

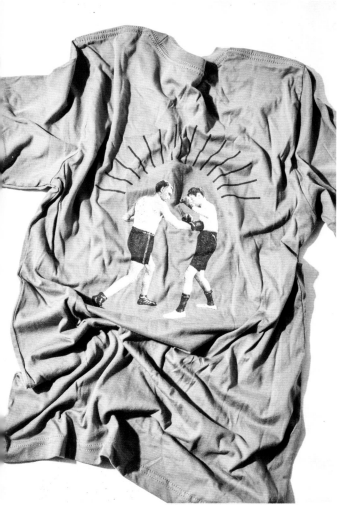

# L'Avenue

Paris, France

**ID** Studio Frisch    **IN** Annvil    **PH** Khalid Zeynalov    **SC** Liene Felsberga (Desktop Publishing)    **CL** Sight Group

The story of L'Avenue revolves around the concept of patrons relishing both fantastic food and the finer things in life amid an elegant setting filled with pockets of lush greenery. For its visual identity, Studio Frisch were inspired by luxurious little details like classic typography paired with glints of golden textures, without overshadowing the overarching artistic yet minimalistic theme of its contemporary interior. The resulting overall look-and-feel of the restaurant is akin to stepping inside a holiday postcard taken at an exotic location, infused with the carefree vibes of a getaway yet grounded in a sense of tradition and familiarity.

# L'Avenue

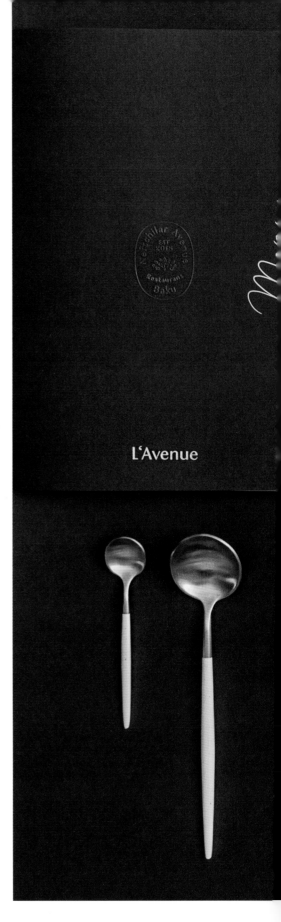

L'Avenue

L'Avenue

Old World red wines

Cote D'OR

Cote de Nuits

Louis Jadot Gevrey-Chambertin 2012
Pinot Noir, Gevrey-Chambertin AC

Albert Bichot Nuits Saint-Georges Les Crots 2009
Pinot Noir, Nuits-Saint-Georges Les Crots 1er Cru AC

Louis Jadot Vosne-Romanee Les Beaux Monts 2011
Pinot Noir, Vosne-Romanee Les Beaux Monts 1er Cru AC

Louis Latour Latricieres-Chambertin Grand Cru 2007
Pinot Noir, Latricieres-Chambertin Grand Cru AC

Romanee Conti, Richebourg Grand Cru 2006
Pinot Noir, Richebourg Grand Cru

Cote de Beaune

Anne Delaroche Hautes Cotes de Beaune Rouge 2014
Pinot Noir, Cotes de Beaune AC

Albert Bichot Aloxe-Corton 2010
Pinot Noir, Aloxe-Corton AC

Louis Latour Pommard 2011
Pinot Noir, Pommard AC

Louis Latour Corton 2006
Pinot Noir, Corton Grand Cru AC

Fleurie 2015

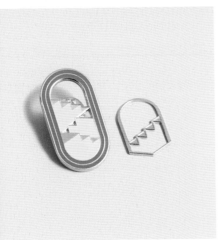

# Botanist

Vancouver, Canada

**ID** Glasfurd & Walker     **IN** Ste. Marie     **PH** Ian Lanternman (Concept), Ema Peters (Interior)     **CL** Botanist Restaurant

Inspired to depict the Pacific Northwest in a whole new way, Glasfurd & Walker created an award-winning visual identity for Botanist retaurant. From design and décor to cocktails and cuisine, the dining destination reflects the vibrant and lush earthiness of the region, with four distinct areas that come together even with their own robust personalities. In bringing the interior's wonder and charm to life, the studio played with the intersection of art and science while carefully considering the context of use and application for each printed piece. Through the thoughtful details, they manifested a juxtaposition and complementary unification of fields – representative of the philosophy throughout the entire venue.

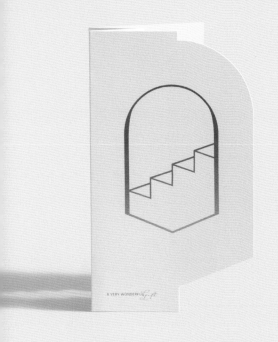

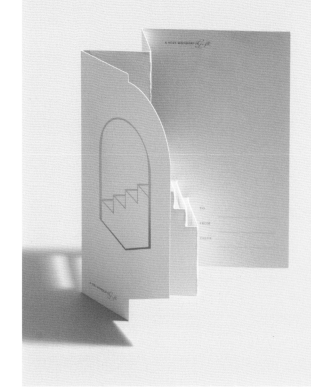

Step inside the Botanist,
a world where day
blurs into night,
summer into winter, and
food and drink are plenty.

BOTANIST

A VERY WONDERFUL Gift

BAR

GARDEN

DINING ROOM

CHAMPAGNE LOUNGE

TO

FROM

VALUE

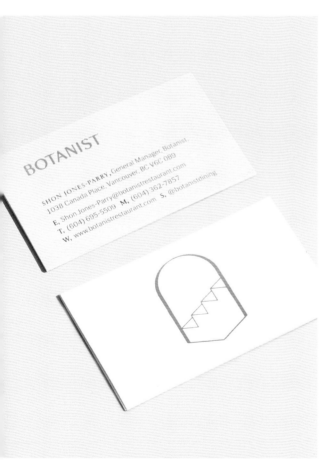

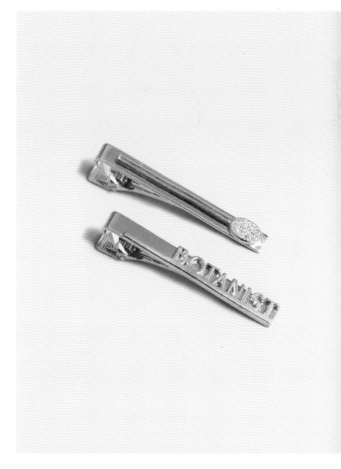

# Le Farfalle

Charleston, USA

**ID** Outline     **IN** David Thompson Architect     **PH** Andrew Cebulka     **CL** Michael & Caitlin Toscano

Renowned chef and restaurant owner Michael Toscano and his wife Caitlin sought to find a balance between complex Italian flavours and a romantic and whimsical aesthetic for their first dining venture in Charleston. Its name, Le Farfalle, was derived from an Italian idiom about chasing butterflies – a notion that inspired Outline to feature an optimistic, custom-lettered wordmark and subtle netted patterns in its visual identity. As an homage to important culinary eras of the past, they took cues from vintage Barilla packaging design to apply charming touches of golden foil that complement the space's green accents.

OSTERIA

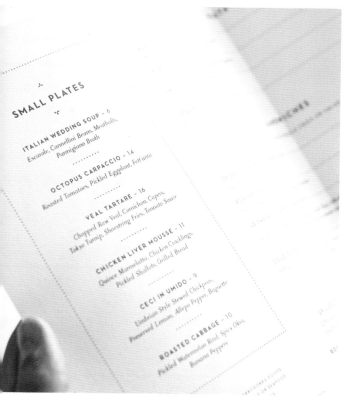

## SMALL PLATES

**ITALIAN WEDDING SOUP** - 6
Escarole, Cannellini Beans, Meatballs,
Parmigiano Broth

**OCTOPUS CARPACCIO** - 14
Roasted Tomatoes, Pickled Eggplant, Fett'unto

**VEAL TARTARE** - 16
Chopped Raw Veal, Cornichon, Capers,
Tokyo Turnips, Shoestring Fries, Tonnato Sauce

**CHICKEN LIVER MOUSSE** - 11
Quince Marmellata, Chicken Cracklings,
Pickled Shallots, Grilled Bread

**CECI IN UMIDO** - 9
Umbrian Style Stewed Chickpeas,
Preserved Lemon, Allepo Pepper, Baguette

**ROASTED CABBAGE** - 10
Pickled Watermelon Rind, Spicy Okra,
Banana Peppers

LEFARFALLECHARLESTON.COM

# Hill of Grace Restaurant

Adelaide, Australia

**ID** Studio Band    **CL** Henschke

### BEERS & CIDERS

| | | |
|---|---|---|
| Hahn Premium Light | NSW | 7.5 |
| Hahn Super Dry | NSW | 9.5 |
| Hahn Super Dry 3.5 | NSW | 8 |
| James Squire Nine Tails Amber Ale | NSW | 9.8 |
| James Squire 150 Lashes Pale Ale | NSW | 9.8 |
| James Squire The Chancer Golden Ale | NSW | 9.8 |
| James Squire Stowaway IPA | NSW | 9.8 |
| James Squire Four Wives Pilsener | NSW | 9.8 |
| James Squire Jack of Spades Porter | NSW | 9.8 |
| Little Creatures Pale Ale | WA | 10.5 |
| Little Creatures Bright Ale | WA | 10.5 |
| Little Creatures Pilsner | WA | 10.5 |
| Kosciuszko Pale Ale | Jindabyne | 12 |
| Corona | Mexico | 11 |
| Heineken | Netherlands | 11 |
| Birra Moretti | Italy | 10 |
| James Squire Orchard Crush Apple Cider | NSW | 10.5 |
| Kirin Fuji Apple Cider | Japan | 12 |

**South Australian Beers**

| | | |
|---|---|---|
| Pikes Sparkling Ale | Clare Valley | 12 |
| Knappstein Lager | Clare Valley | 12 |
| HVB Bee Sting | Barossa Valley | 12 |
| Goodieson Wheat Beer | McLaren Vale | 12 |
| Lobethal Chocolate Oatmeal Stout | Lobethal | 12 |

Henschke, a renowned Adelaide wine label, branched out with a restaurant located in the historic Adelaide Oval called Hill of Grace. To highlight the eatery's delightful food and wine menu as well as the iconic area itself, Studio Band redefined its brand by establishing a stronger connection with the area. On top of using photography to create a visual parallel between meaningful subjects such as footy boots with gumboots and a 1950s pitch roller with an old Henschke truck, they updated the uniform, signage, as well as the logotype – using a bespoke typeface based on the classic lettering on the Adelaide Oval scoreboard.

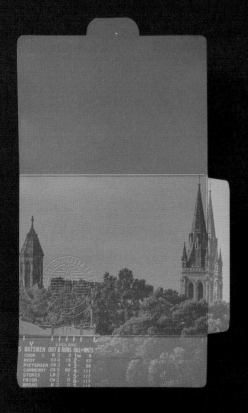

**FOUR COURSE**

**STARTERS**

**Ortlieb Chicken Tails and Leather Jacket Cheeks,** *Oyster Puree, Beef Tendon, Salmon Roe, Smoots Leaves*

**Port Lincoln Octopus,** *Pork Bacon, Smoked Bacon Bone Puree, Rye Sourdough Skin, Oregano*

**Paroo Kangaroo Tartare,** *Tat-tin Flavours Fava's Milk, Puff Cheese, Soil Roasted Beetroot, Bullfoil Leaf*

**Raw Hiramasa Kingfish,** *Strathmond Valley Dattes Coconut Yoghurt, Fermented Kale Coconut Granita, Mandarin, Ginger, Preserved Lime Leaf*

**ENTRÉE**

**Roasted Blackhawk Carrots,** *Local Masons Carrot Gel, Goats Curd, Carrot Jus, Black Dirt*

**Coorong Wild Seafood Mullet,** *Warm Raw and Butter Sea Lamb, Salted Egg, Pickled Onions, Port Lincoln Sardine Custard*

**Tasig, Curled Pork,** *Spring Onion, Soft Egg*

**SA Baby Squid,** *Lemon & Seaweed, Thyme, Fennel Coffee Bay Oyster and Mushroom Broth*

**MAIN**

**Robert's Intermittently,** *Moringa Leaves, Zephfair, Nasturtia, Kritsonicha Mussel and Spring Onion Broth*

**Milk Braised Murray Land Lamb Neck,** *Braised Milk Curds, Broccolini, Native Nut and Lentils Cheese Puree*

**Adelee Shorthorn Beef Cheek,** *Grilled Adelee Fresh Oyster Mushrooms, Garlinck Fresh, Marbles and Quandolings, Crispy Pig Ears*

**Angus Pure Carbonorde Spice Rubbed Beef Fillet,** *Slow Cooked Potato, Coffee and Burnt Jus, Kikloga Kale*

**Chicken, Winter Melon and Dried Prunes,** *Braised Chicken Jus, Crispy Skin*

**Macro Meats Venison,** *Cauliflower Puree, Turkey Flat Pickles, Caramelized Onion*

**SIDES (NOT A MANI)**

**Local Mushrooms,** *Café De Paris Butter, Lemon Thyme Salt*

**Adelaide Hills Brussels Sprouts,** *Barnsdburg Smoked Mustard, Sweet Onion*

**Mixed Leaves & Herb Salad,** *Citrus, Mona Mte Pear's Verjus a Wemcha Oil Dressing*

**DESSERT**

**Mandarin Mousse,** *Bations Of Mandarine, Chocolate Dacquoise*

**Chocolate Brownie,** *Hana Me White Peach and Nashi Pear, Pear Ice Cream, Meringue*

**Toasted Hazelnut Sour Dough,** *Beer & Nut Dough Ice Cream, Frosted Brown, Hazelbts Pear's Verjus, Jelly Onion Custard, Marshmallow*

**Coconut Mousse,** *Tapioca Pearls, Banana Cake*

**Local Cheese,** *Maverick, Lavosh*

# Dotorii

Goyang, South Korea

**ID** Jaeho Shin   **CL** Dotorii

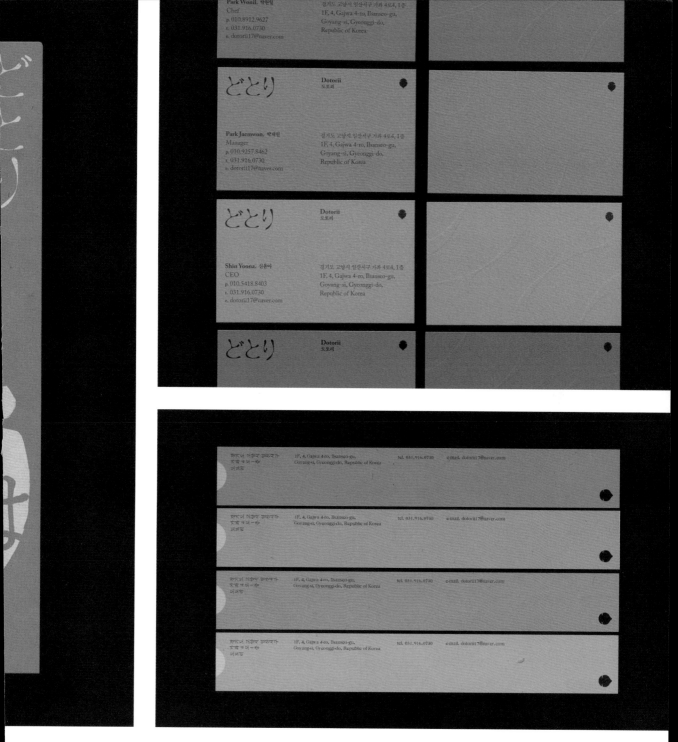

Dotorii is a Korean word that refers to the bud of a young acorn tree. In designing the visual identity for a restaurant named after it, Jaeho Shin was inspired to express the word in the Japanese language – using the hiragana in the logo to subtly depict the process of a shoot sprouting and growing. He also applied the shape of an acorn in white on top of the muted and earthy overall palette to provide a constrasting backdrop on which the delicate typography could be featured. The resulting effect across the restaurant's printed materials is an elegant, cohesive, and impactful branding suite.

どとり

どとり

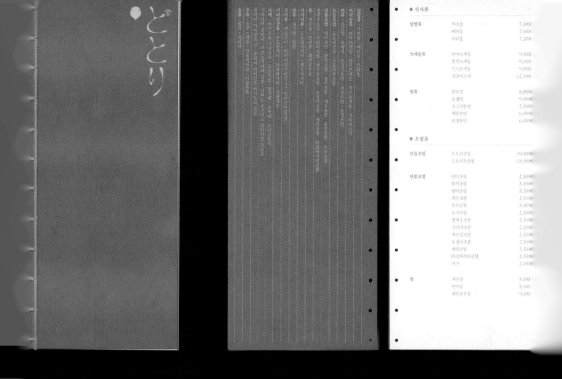

● 식사류

| 덮밥류 | | |
|---|---|---|
| | 자츠동 | 7,000 |
| | 해물동 | 7,000 |
| | 부타동 | 7,500 |
| 쓰께동류 | 언어쓰께동 | 9,000 |
| | 붕작쓰께동 | 9,000 |
| | 믹스쓰께동 | 9,000 |
| | 지라이스사 | 12,000 |
| 면류 | 판모밀 | 8,000 |
| | 초생면 | 9,000 |
| | 소고기우연 | 7,000 |
| | 계란온면 | 6,000 |
| | 오뎅온면 | 6,000 |

● 초밥류

| 모듬초밥 | 도도리초밥 | 10,000 |
|---|---|---|
| | 도도리즉초밥 | 18,000 |
| 단품초밥 | 언어초밥 | 2,500 |
| | 참치초밥 | 3,800 |
| | 장어초밥 | 3,500 |
| | 새우초밥 | 2,500 |
| | 유부군밥 | 3,000 |
| | 소라초밥 | 2,500 |
| | 빗새우초밥 | 2,500 |
| | 가리비초밥 | 2,500 |
| | 새우알초밥 | 2,500 |
| | 오징어초밥 | 2,500 |
| | 계란초밥 | 2,500 |
| | 다김어지미군밥 | 3,500 |
| | 마끼 | 2,000 |
| 롤 | 새우롤 | 8,000 |
| | 언어롤 | 8,000 |
| | 레인보우롤 | 9,000 |

# Graze

Melbourne, Australia

**ID** Madison Tierney     **CL** Graze Wine Bar & Delicatessen

Graze is a wine bar and delicatessen that embodies the spirit of the classic Italian 'enoteche' – a local wine shop that doubles up as the place to meet with friends over a bottle or a plate of prosciutto. In reflecting its mission to inspire confidence in the community by providing uncomplicated, high-quality wine and produce, Madison Tierney created a visual identity that was inspired by the original delicatessens, bars, and wine taverns in Europe around the 1700s. Instead of aerial shots of highly stylised food and wood-cut typography, homage is paid to the dark tones and imagery of 16th and 17th-century still life – complemented by the use of the Gothic Blackletter script that was common from the 11th to the 18th century.

graze

Wine Bar + Delicatessen

180 High St, Northcote
No. 9486 4455
www.graze.com.au

graze

Wine Bar + Delicatessen.

You can find us at —

180 High St, Northcote
No. 9486 4455
www.graze.com.au

graze

Wine Bar + Delicatessen.

You can find us at —

180 High St, Northcote
No. 9486 4455
www.graze.com.au

## bubble 004

| | Bottle | Carafe |
|---|---|---|
| ...ll Tasmanian Cuvée | 80 | 35 |
| ...ahaye Millesime | 300 | N/A |
| ...e Vineyards | 66 | 30 |
| ...'Brut Réserve' | 85 | 40 |
| ...'Complantée' Brut | 99 | 50 |
| ...ahaye 'Violane' | 250 | N/A |
| ...arris 'The Sabre' | 90 | 20 |
| ...Vincent Bérèche | 180 | 60 |
| ...vee Prestige | 380 | N/A |

| | Bottle | Carafe |
|---|---|---|
| ...Pucino Prosecco | 60 | 20 |
| ...go 'Col Fondo' | 97 | 34 |
| ...ra 'Nino' Pet Nat | 60 | 16 |

| | Bottle | Carafe |
|---|---|---|
| ...bais | 145 | 72 |
| ...rrier 'Cuvée Rosé' | 80 | 40 |
| ...dswick 'Brut Rosé' | 300 | N/A |
| ...che Demi-Sec | 100 | 50 |

## white 004

| | Bottle | Carafe |
|---|---|---|
| ...indi 'Block 6' Vintage | 230 | N/A |
| ...Hunter Gatherer Vintners | 90 | 45 |
| Bellvale 'Quercus' Vineyard | 70 | 35 |
| Mahana Estate Gravity | 90 | 45 |

| | Bottle | Carafe |
|---|---|---|
| Yabby Lake Vineyard | 75 | 37 |
| Jr. Jones | 280 | N/A |
| Voyager Estate 'Girt by Sea' | 60 | 30 |

| | Bottle | Carafe |
|---|---|---|
| The Story 'Whitelands Close Planted' | 70 | 24 |
| Xabregas 'Figtree' | 84 | 42 |
| Keller 'Von der Fels' | 135 | N/A |
| Joh. Joh. Prüm Kabinett 'Graacher' | 80 | 40 |
| Nikolaihof 'Vom Stein' Federspiel | 60 | 32 |

| | Bottle | Carafe |
|---|---|---|
| Château Mourgues Grès Blanc | 71 | 35 |
| Quinta do Ameal Loureiro | 90 | 45 |
| La Caña Albariño | 60 | 30 |
| Fratelli D'Anna Vernaccia blend | 82 | 41 |

## red 004

| | Bottle | Carafe |
|---|---|---|
| ...awford River Cabernet Merlot | 80 | 40 |
| ...re a Terra Cabernet Sauvignon | 98 | 50 |
| ...rager Estate 'Girt by Sea' Cabernet Merlot | 90 | 45 |
| ...teau Cos d' Estournel Saint Estèphe 2nd | 760 | N/A |
| ...side Valley Estate | 66 | 23 |
| ...n Vanya Cabernet Sauvignon | 40 | 20 |

| | Bottle | Carafe |
|---|---|---|
| ...Langi Ghiran 'Cliff Edge' | 120 | 60 |
| ...h 'The Schubert Theorem' | 140 | 70 |
| ...l-Saint-Joseph 'The Common Good' | 100 | 50 |
| ...a 'Hilltops' Shiraz | 60 | 30 |
| ...'The Steading' blend | 45 | 23 |

| | | Bottle | Carafe |
|---|---|---|---|
| | ...arone della Valpolicella Corvina | 60 | 30 |
| | ...'Figtree' | 84 | 42 |
| | ...der Fels' | 135 | N/A |
| | ...um Kabinett 'Graacher' | 120 | 60 |
| | ...om Stein' Federspiel | 64 | 32 |
| | ...tops 'Sete di Vino' Primitivo | 80 | 40 |
| | ...yllabus of Eros' Nero d'Avola | 360 | 180 |
| 2010 | Two by Two Sangiovese/Cabernet Sauvignon | 200 | 100 |
| 2012 | Montevecchio 'Rosse' Multi-Varietal | 40 | 20 |

## plate 004

| | Smaller |
|---|---|
| | 6 |
| ..., Oregano, Thyme, Rosemary Salted Butter | 8 |
| ...h Wholemeal Toast | 5 |
| ..., preserved Zucchini | 6 |
| ...Asparagus | 9 |
| | 8 |
| ...e Half Shell with Mignonette Ice | 16 |
| | 10 |

| | Cheese |
|---|---|
| ...n Cow/Sheep blend, Oat Crisp Bread | 12 |
| ...ps Milk, Burnt Onion Marmalade | 16 |
| ...Cheese, Pickled Plums | 12 |
| ...oked Cow's milk Cheese, Walnuts | 10 |
| ...ert, Chestnuts, Rosemary, Ciabatta Toast | 18 |
| ...house Cheddar, Hard Cow's milk | 12 |
| ...ried Fruits | 10 |

| | Meats |
|---|---|
| ...o De Bellota, Free Range Acorn fed Ham 20g | 10 |
| ...Thick and Dried Pork Sausage 20g | 12 |
| ...Di San Daniele, Sweet and Aromatic 15g | 20 |
| ...Cured Pork Cold Cut 10g | 8 |
| ...d Sausage with Wheat Toast 25g | 18 |
| ...Cured Pork Tenderloin 15g | 16 |
| ...rizo 20g | 10 |

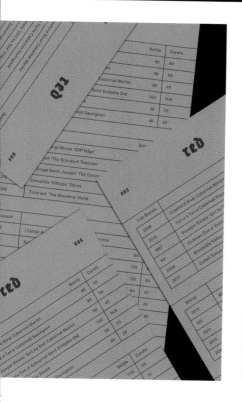

# East Village

Sydney, Australia

ID The Colour Club    CL East Village Sydney

Cellar by the glass, Work i

Manzanilla I Think Sher

Sparkling Viognier Dubst

Brachetto d'Soumah Frizzant

Pittnauer Blaufrankish Ro

Savvy B Skinnydip!

Le Petit Mort Viognier Am

Pinot Noir Label Corsic

Garnatxa Alta Alella

Cahors K'Or

After years of abandonment and a handful of failed refurbishment attempts, the bloodhouse of Tilly Devine, a notoriously ruthless madam in the 1920s, was finally reinstated into a sophisticated dining and drinking destination known as East Village Sydney. Sprawling over three levels, it offers an urban and minimal wine-focused bar on the first floor, a sports club with dark tones and worn leather seating on the second floor, as well as the jewel in the crown: a rooftop terrace with incredible cocktails and city views. Playing with simple yet clearly distinguishable typography and colour systems, The Colour Club created distinctions across each level whilst maintaining a sense of cohesiveness throughout the striking visual identity.

# Puebla 109

Mexico City, Mexico

**ID** Savvy Studio     **IN** Marcela Lugo, Arturo Dib     **SC** Marcos Castro, Lucía Oceguera, Juan Caloca, Luis Alberú

Puebla 109 is a restaurant and bar in Mexico City's vibrant Roma Norte neighbourhood where art, design, and gastronomy converge. Deriving inspiration from the classic age of Mexican philately, Savvy Studio developed a unique visual identity around key symbols resembling stamps that work independently and yet share an equal hierarchy when placed together. They also complemented the venue's cosy setting where natural materials meet industrial accents with bold colours and typefaces that have strong connections to local culture; evoking warm authenticity and the nostalgic charm that comes from reminiscing about life and the postal service in the past.

# Interiors & Architecture

Visualising brands in space

2WEEKS

Bibo

Campo Modern Grill

Dinette Bistro & Bar

Foxglove

Hikari

Icha Chateau

Kaikaya

Madison Beauty Salon

Mrs. Pound

NANAN Patisserie

Omar's Place

Papillon Bar & Restaurant

Paradis

PORT2.0

PUNKRAFT

RAW

Restaurant Kompaniya

The Ocean

Tunateca Balfegó

Xiaoyouyu Seafood Restaurant

Human beings are fundamentally sensorial and emotional creatures. Although eating and drinking can be seen as mere necessities in life that do not require much fanfare, the right setting can elevate even the most mundane of everyday activities to an extraordinary and memorable experience. In creating the best atmosphere for every patron, restaurant and bar interiors and architecture need to be in perfect harmony with their visual identities as the vessels for meaningful moments. Thanks to social media today, successful spaces can also draw attention before one even tries out their menus – as exemplified by the following projects.

# Omar's Place

London, United Kingdom

**IN & ID** Sella Concept    **AR** Wilson Holloway (Consultation)    **PH** Nicholas Worley
**SC** Carl Hansen, Note Design Studio, D'Armes, Pool (Furniture Design)    **CL** Omar's Place

For Omar's Place, a creative tapas kitchen and contemporary cocktail bar with the convivial atmosphere of a local hangout, Sella Concept sought to bring together its sophisticated menu and welcoming ambience. Deriving inspiration from the Mediterranean lifestyle, the region's fresh produce, as well as the owner's background, they based their creative concept on the sun – making it the core element of the venue's visual identity and interior design. Paired with Wilson Holloway's distinctly Milanese aesthetic in terms of material choices and colour palettes, the outcome exudes character and charm.

# The Ocean

Hong Kong, Hong Kong

**IN & ID** A Work of Substance    **PH** Dennis Lo    **CL** Le Comptoir Group

More than just a restaurant and cocktail lounge, The Ocean stands out as a timeless architectural landmark against the dramatic vistas of Repulse Bay in Hong Kong. By featuring floor-to-ceiling windows that greet patrons with the ever-changing beauty of its namesake, sleek lines reminiscent of a classic schooner, as well as customised furnishings like hand-blown glass lights and 'living' aquarium walls, A Work of Substance added a contemporary-chic edge to an inherently elegant fine-dining establishment. Besides utilising a multitude of textures, they also infused elements from the surrounding urban and natural landscapes to create a cohesive sensorial journey.

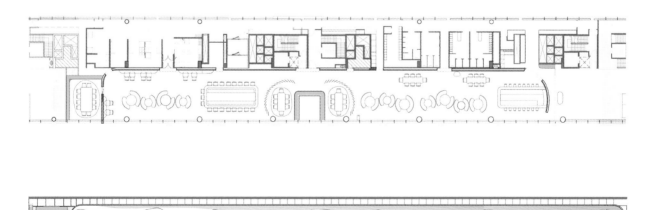

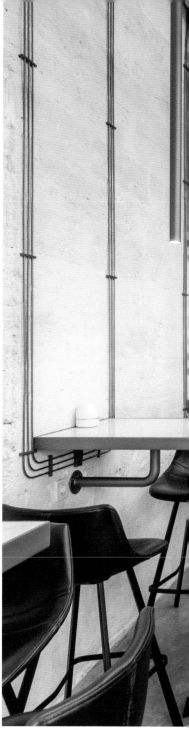

# Madison Beauty Salon

Odessa, Ukraine

**IN** YøDezeen Architects    **PH** Shurpenkov Andrii    **CL** Madison Beauty Salon

Besides what its name suggests, Madison Beauty Salon in Odessa also serves as a bar. Instead of a luxurious and intimidating setting, YøDezeen Architects designed a stylish yet cosy interior, making the most of the high ceilings and exposed walls from the original construction to create a sense of effortless grandeur. Amid the base tones of black and white, copper elements function as accents against the cement, granite, and marble surfaces, highlighting an existing arch they also chose to retain as a feature. Complementary materials and fixtures such as the cantilever table tops and terracotta velvet curtains set the tone further for the chic and unique space.

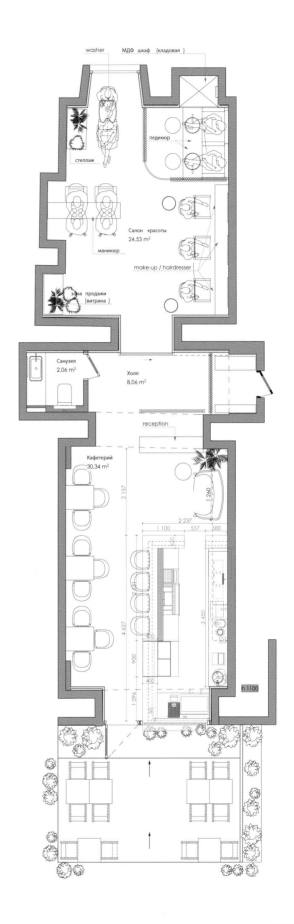

# Campo Modern Grill

Wroclaw, Poland

**IN & ID** BUCK.STUDIO     **PH** PION Basia Kuligowska, Przemysław Nieciecki     **CL** KB FOOD&CATERING

Simplicity and sincerity are the main features of both CAMPO Modern Grill's culinary offerings and BUCK.STUDIO's interior design work. The natural materials and dark colours used within the spacious restaurant reflect the honesty and respect with which ingredients are chosen and subsequently prepared – values that also come to life through its functional zoned layout, fully-glazed transparent surfaces, as well as its own namesake, which translates to 'a field' in the Ibero-American languages. Far from creating a stiff and spiritless ambience, its wood, brass, leather, and neon elements work together to form a warm and homely setting where patrons can enjoy hearty Argentine steaks and an authentic menu with South American highlights.

# 2WEEKS

Beirut, Lebanon

**IN** Rabih Geha Architects    **PH** Tony Elieh    **CL** ADDMIND Group

Overlooking Beirut's seaport, the interiors of 2WEEKS were based on the concept of containment without caging. Inspired to create 'a shell within a shell', Rabih Geha Architects worked closely with their clients to bring their unique vision for the indoor club to life. Its 'webbed shell' framework was designed to complement the linear lighting elements and colour palette throughout the space to create a cocoon-like ambience. Using a combination of materials, craftsmanship, and visual communication, they provided club-goers with an immersive experience that transported them into another world.

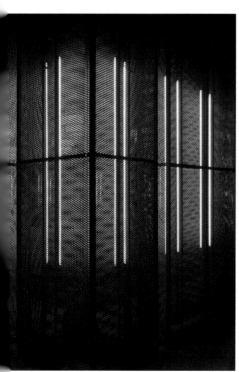

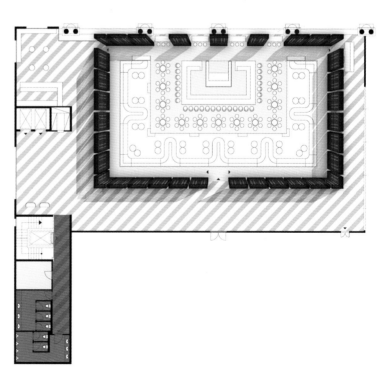

# Bibo

Hong Kong, Hong Kong

**IN & ID** A Work of Substance  **PH** Nathaniel McMahon  **CL** Le Comptoir Group

A Work of Substance were challenged to realise an intriguing restaurant concept where modern street art and classic French gastronomy could co-exist in harmony. Deriving inspiration from the flexible and flair-filled design aesthetics of 1930s Art Deco, they transformed the interior of a discreet old building in a quiet neighbourhood into Bibo, a distinctive new setting for exciting culinary experiences and eclectic artistic expression. As the creative foundation for the physical space, they also invented a compelling brand story in which an abandoned French tram company office was taken over by a colony of street artists who would layer and tag their ideas on any surface with a history.

COMPAGNIE
GENERALE
FRANÇAISE
●
DE TRAMWAYS

BiBO $220

DR. ORDINAIRE'S ELIXIR

THE ABSINTHE RECIPE WAS CREATED BY DR. ORDINAIRE IN
1792 IN RURAL FRANCE, SHORTLY AFTER THE FRENCH
REVOLUTION. AS TRAVELED AROUND THE VAL DE TRAVERS ON
HIS FAITHFUL HORSE ROCKET AND SOLD HIS ABSINTHE
INITIALLY AS AN ALL-PURPOSE CURE-ALL. A 136 PROOF
ELIXIR.

LA FOLIE VERTE                                           $180

LIFE WITHOUT ABSINTHE? I CANNOT IMAGINE IT! FOR ME IT
WOULD BE IMPOSSIBLE! I SHOULD HANG, DROWN OR SHOOT
MYSELF INTO INFINITUDE. OUT OF SHEER RAGE AT THE
CONTINUED CRUELTY AND INJUSTICE OF THE WORLD - BUT
WITH THIS BEING NECTAR OF OLYMPUS I CAN DEFY
MISFORTUNE. LONG LIFE TO YOUR HEALTH, MON BRAVE! DRINK
WITH ME.

DANGEROUS ATTRACTION                                    $130

# Dinette Bistro & Bar

Wroclaw, Poland

**IN & ID** BUCK.STUDIO     **PH** PION Basia Kuligowska, Przemysław Nieciecki     **CL** Food Concept

Dinette Bistro & Bar provides patrons with a casual atmosphere to tuck into classic seasonal dishes amid distinctive interiors inspired by Polish mid-century modern design. For its third branch located in Wroclaw Old Town, BUCK.STUDIO merged all of the most charming and characteristic elements of the restaurant's previous ventures to create a chic yet cosy setting for open and memorable gatherings, featuring a lively green hue, wooden touches, marble counters, and chequered floor surfaces. The creamy grey walls and various custom-made furniture add to the communal vibes of the space, which takes it cues from the French bistronomy movement in the past.

# Restaurant Kompaniya

Saint Petersburg, Russia

**IN** DA. Design & Architecture    **PH** Sergey Melnikov    **CL** Restaurant Kompaniya

DA. Design & Architecture set out to create a contemporary yet cosy overall atmosphere for the fourth Kompaniya project by renowned restauranteurs Aleksei Krylov and Aleksandr Prokofev in Saint Petersburg. Although its original layout was complicated to begin with, they successfully organised the venue in a cohesive manner by reflecting the brand's classic aesthetics in one section, and transforming another into a winter garden with outdoor furniture, spotlights, and planters. They also utilised the double-height ceilings and tall windows to add lightness to the space and accentuate the connection between its two levels.

# NANAN Patisserie

Wroclaw, Poland

**IN & ID** BUCK.STUDIO     **PH** PION Basia Kuligowska, Przemysław Nieciecki     **CL** Justyna Kawiak, Barbara Migdal-Brzozowska

NANAN is a patisserie that embodies its namesake – which means 'sweetmeats' in French – through its tempting treats and dreamy décor. Instead of basing their work on a 'safe' concept by taking creative cues from typical confectionery designs, BUCK.STUDIO deliberately chose an unexpected, minimal-chic aesthetic for the space to draw attention to the finely decorated cakes and pastries on display in jeweller-inspired glass cabinets. Using a combination of pink velvet walls, arched doorways, delicate brass details, subtle lighting, and bespoke interior fixtures, they created a sophisticated yet surreal world that brings art and sweets together in a surprising and delightful way.

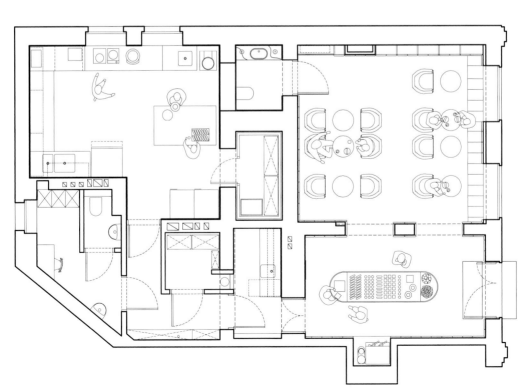

# Kaikaya

Valencia, Spain

**IN** Masquespacio    **PH** Luis Beltran    **CL** Kaikaya

A compelling fusion of Japanese elements and Brazilian tropicalismo, Kaikaya merges two unique cultures with strong identities for Valencia's first tropical sushi restaurant. To reflect the right mix of methodical and exotic influences, Masquespacio's initial work revolved around the venue itself

– retaining its vaults, metallic beams, and original bricks to highlight the beauty of imperfections left over time. They then added bold coloured patterns representative of both countries, warm materials like raffia and wood as a nod to its Asian heritage, eclectic yet emblematic fixtures, as well as lots of greenery to create a contemporary-boho botanical paradise.

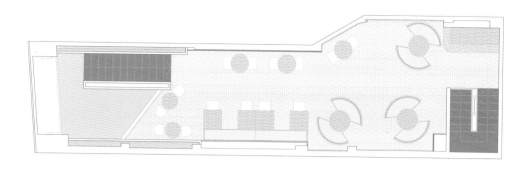

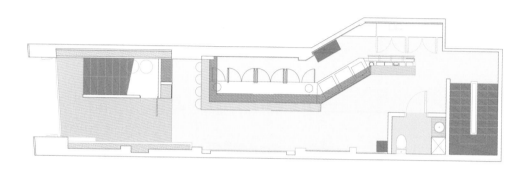

# Tunateca Balfegó

Barcelona, Spain

**IN** El Equipo Creativo    **ID** C43Crea_Rafel Codina Filbà    **LT** Artec3 Studio    **PH** Adrià Goula
**SC** Àlex Torralba (Engineering), Fran Fernández (Acoustic Engineering)    **CL** Balfegó Group

In promoting red tuna as a quality product, Tunateca Balfegó has become an important communication platform for the Balfegó family. Within its dining space, El Equipo Creativo created three zones to reflect the fish's different aspects and stages of its capture: the undulating BLUE ROOM representing the depths of the sea, the almost-clinical yet irregular shape-filled RONQUEO ROOM where traditional manual dissections of tuna take place, as well as two cosy PRIVATE ROOMS inspired by the meat of red tuna itself. The clever mix of materials and finishing touches, such as wooden tables with reddish hues and visible streaks that form the subtle outline of a golden fishbone, offer patrons a unique sensorial experience rooted in seafood.

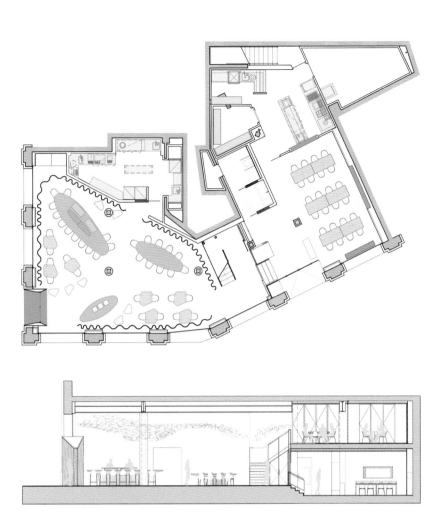

# Hikari

Valencia, Spain

**IN** Masquespacio    **PH** Luis Beltran    **CL** Hikari

Masquespacio were inspired by the maze of hidden alleys and quarters in Tokyo, a city where countless yakitori bars are nestled, to bring the concept of Hikari to life. Combining concrete surfaces, wooden components, and rusty metallic finishes with clever spatial planning and lighting design, they juxtaposed industrial materials with familiar urban touches to evoke the sights, smells, and sounds of izakaya-lined streets. Combined with the menu, the striking overall visual impact treats patrons to an authentic yakitori dining experience.

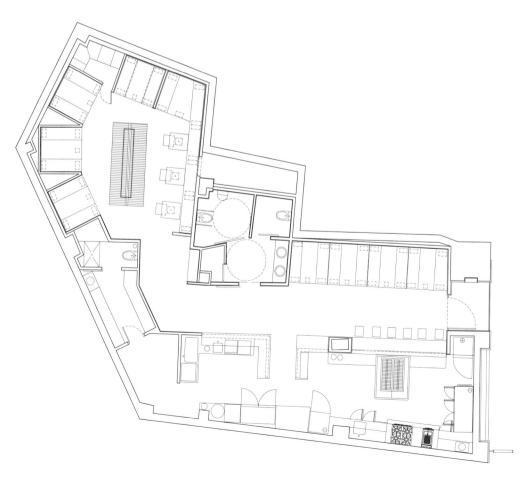

# Icha Chateau

Shanghai, China

**IN** Spacemen    **PH** Min Chen Xuan    **CL** Icha Group

Spacemen looked to the rolling hills of tea plantations to inform the design for Icha Chateau's flagship restaurant and tea bar in Shanghai. Inspired by the structure of the mid-19th century colonial heritage building in which it is housed, they created an undulating sculptural installation made out of 35,000-m gold chains to form a scenic visual landscape. Besides carving out partitions and private areas, the resulting organic shapes also contrast with the contemporary materials used throughout the space, such as the grey terrazzo marble floor, matte black cabinetry, and brass orbs of light that follow the curves of the chain curtains, to create a scenic topography that highlights their innovative take on a traditional institution.

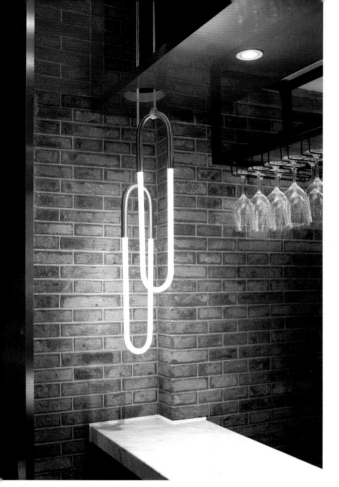

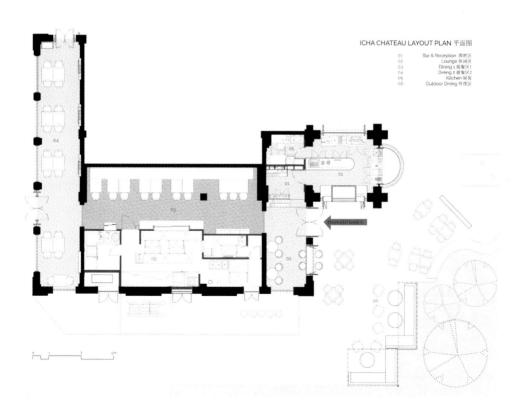

ICHA CHATEAU LAYOUT PLAN 平面图

01    Bar & Reception 酒吧区
02    Lounge 休闲区
03    Dining 1 就餐区1
04    Dining 2 就餐区2
05    Kitchen 厨房
06    Outdoor Dining 外摆区

MAIN ENTRANCE

# PUNKRAFT

Kyiv, Ukraine

**IN** ater.architects    **ID** hooga.design    **PH** Andrey Avdeenko    **SC** Alexander Grebenyuk (Wall Art Design)

Situated right around the corner of a historical pedestrian street in downtown Kyiv is PUNKRAFT, a craft beer bar. For its interiors, ater.architects were inspired by the industrial aesthetics of beer equipment and the philosophies of the craft brewing movement to depict freedom, experimentation, custom production, and all things punk. In realising their concept, they combined stainless steel, rolled metal, concrete, wood, and neon with lively illustrations to create an atmosphere brimming with attitude. They also retained and restored the original brick arches of the site to maintain the sense of authenticity within the space.

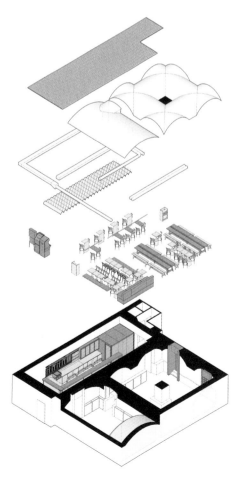

# Mrs. Pound

Hong Kong, Hong Kong

**IN** NC Design & Architecture Ltd (NCDA)    **ID** NCDA, a107, Entendre Studios    **PH** Dennis Lo Designs, Justin Lim

A speakeasy bar disguised as an old Chinese stamp shop, Mrs. Pound puts a modern and playful spin on Asian fusion. Basing their work on an underlying fictional narrative of two star-crossed lovers who use the shop as their clandestine meeting spot, NC Design & Architecture designed a multilayered sensorial and gastronomical experience using a synthesis of atmospheric details. From the secret stamp-activated concealed door to the vibrant pink dining room filled with vintage photos, kitsch memorabilia, and hybrid finishes blending glamorous feminine touches with rugged masculine accents, the studio were inspired by cult classics like Wong Kar-Wai's 'In the Mood for Love' to realise the characters' mysterious and extravagant lives.

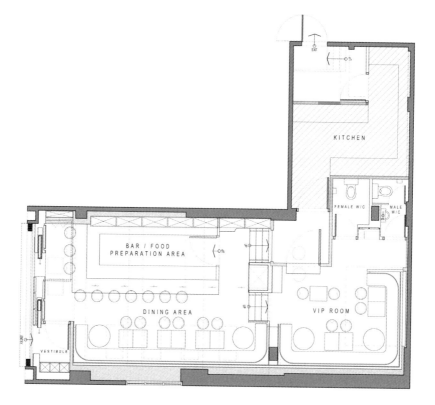

# PORT 2.0

Saint Petersburg, Russia

**ID** DA. Design & Architecture    **PH** Sergey Melnikov    **CL** Restaurant PORT 2.0

To illustrate the beauty of the Northern fishing ports and ships in Saint Petersburg, DA. Design & Architecture fused the effects of brutality and simplicity for PORT2.0's interiors. Instead of going down the expected route with a marine-driven theme, their concept for the seafood restaurant revolved around a raw industrial style and Scandinavian minimalism. To complement the massive concrete columns, metal piping, and wooden elements within the space, they added custom-made lighting fixtures such as netted chandeliers and jellyfish lamps, as well as a stainless steel full-wall mural with a carved fish pattern as a contemporary chic nod to its nautical surroundings.

# Papillon Bar & Restaurant

Athens, Greece

**IN** Minas Kosmidis   **PH** Ioanna Roufopoulou

For Papillon, an all-day restaurant and bar located in the Northern Athenian suburb of Neo Psychiko, Minas Kosmidis were inspired by the bistro culture of Paris and New York from the Belle Époque to the Jazz Age eras in conceptualising its interiors.

Upon entering the establishment, patrons are welcomed by hardwood floors, floral wallpaper, and tall coffered ceilings that set the scene for a memorable experience. An eclectic selection of artwork adds a playful note to the classic and chic aesthetics, complementing the brass, leather, marble, and walnut wood surfaces that exude a sense of luxurious comfort.

# Foxglove

Hong Kong, Hong Kong

**IN & ID** NC Design & Architecture Ltd (NCDA)    **PH** Dennis Lo Designs

Bringing together two quintessential elements of British heritage, namely the finest handcrafted umbrellas and the traditional private members' club, Foxglove is a 4,300-sqf fantasy world inspired by the globe-trotting adventures of an English gentleman. Upon entering a secret door in an elegant umbrella boutique filled with bespoke brass-edged cabinets, patrons are welcomed into the restaurant and bar's exclusive inner sanctum that drips with vintage luxury and first-class glamour. Besides offering them the age-old pleasure of discovering hidden surprises in intimate spaces, NC Design & Architecture's work also features exquisite materials, moody palettes, and cinematic touches to lend a distinct allure to the venue itself.

# Xiaoyouyu Seafood Restaurant

Xiamen, China

**IN** Xiamen Fancy Design & Decoration Co., Ltd    **PH** Jin Weiqi    **CL** Xiaoyouyu Seafood Restaurant

Traditional seafood stalls are generally known to be messy and crowded. In breaking this stereotype, Xiamen Fancy Design & Decoration went down a different path for Xiaoyouyu Seafood Restaurant's interiors by featuring an artwork-like entrance, serpentine circulations, warm wooden textures, and artificial natural landscapes to set the tone for tranquility. As a former factory terrace, the unique location and unconventional structure made the perfect backdrop for design play and experimentation, resulting in the creation of various visual stimuli for more interesting and meaningful dining experiences. Through the interconnected yet multilayered venue, they built an other-worldly spatial narrative that is both enriching and inspiring.

# RAW

Taipei, Taiwan

**IN** WEIJENBERG  **PH** mwphotoinc  **CL** Chef André Chiang for RAW, Taipei, Taiwan

The collaboration between chef André Chiang's vivid gastronomic imagination and WEIJENBERG's artistic vision defined RAW's visceral restaurant interiors by telling a tale parallel to the epicurean experience. Patrons would begin their journey by crossing a wooden path into a tranquil lounge – a gentle transition away from the bustling streets of Taipei. They would then be drawn toward an undulating wooden sculpture that encircles the dining area and forms the centrepiece of the venue, with tailor-made furniture, textural finishes, and thoughtful lighting design further setting the scene.

kitchen.
*noun*

This is a kitchen. A place for creativity, a place to dream. Dream to be brave. Never to be afraid of making mistakes. Always questioning the possibilities, never sitting still, but always evolving and pushing ourselves. We will respect the past and never forget where we came from. Humility is our key ingredient. We are here not to feed the stomach but to fill the heart and soul.

It's not about the country or the culture, it's about the state of mind.

If this is a dream please don't wake me up – George Calombaris

# Paradis

Hong Kong, Hong Kong

**IN & ID** A Work of Substance     **PH** Dennis Lo     **CL** Matthieu Lemoine

Drawing upon ancient Haitian voodoo practices, A Work of Substance were inspired by the Goddess of the Moon in designing Paradis's visual identity and interiors. The studio sought to capture the mesmerising and mystical qualities of a lunar eclipse through the rich greens, earthy browns, and striking golden finishes that formed the basis of the restaurant and bar's deep and alluring colour palette. Besides allowing creatures of the night to see their deepest animalistic desires reflected in the hand-painted wall murals, the venue's low ceilings and material combinations also set the mood by forming a warm cocoon in which they could revel in new discoveries and secrets.

# EXPERT TALK

on brand applications and interiors

———

## VISUAL IDENTITY

Max Dautresme, A Work of Substance
Phoebe Glasfurd & Aren Fieldwalker, Glasfurd & Walker

## INTERIOR DESIGN

Fedor Goreglyad, Boris Lvovskiy, Maria Romanova & Anna Lvovskaia,
DA. Design & Architecture
Ana Milena Hernández Palacios & Christophe Penasse, Masquespacio

———

# A Work of Substance

———

Dialogue with Founding Partner
Max Dautresme

Driven by imagination and ideas that push boundaries, A Work of Substance dedicates itself to doing and offering exactly what its name stands for in every project. Although the studio's commissions span the globe, its passion lies in its base, Hong Kong; where it uses design as a meaningful tool to reinvigorate culture and local neighbourhoods across a multitude of touchpoints that include branding for restaurants and bars. In the following interview, BRANDLife speaks to founding partner Max Dautresme about his inspiration and not responding to trends even amid an ever-changing F&B landscape.

**Why are effective visual identities important in a dining and drinking experience?**

So many of life's memorable moments take place in restaurants, and the way we remember what happened has everything to do with the sense of place and atmosphere: the scents, the colours, the flavours… Visual identities are important because they translate the craft that happens in the kitchen and bar. The visual stimulation helps to complete a backdrop for experiences that people will remember and get inspired by.

**A Work of Substance's portfolio encompasses a variety of clients. What are some of the best restaurant or bar briefs you have ever received?**

Bibo came with a complex brief, which made it interesting. There was a big contrast between the rawness of the space and the refined gastronomy it serves. We needed to come up with a formula that would ensure that these elements existed in harmony and worked together as a whole.

**What inspires your creative output?**

Travelling helps me keep my sense of curiosity. When I travel, I get inspired because my routine is broken, which makes me more aware, and this heightened awareness increases my appreciation for my surroundings. Also, thorough research to understand the product, the location, and the audience of a project helps to distil the essence on which the design should be built upon.

**How would you like customers to enjoy and experience your work?**

Our goal is to make you the last guest to leave. We ask ourselves how we would want customers to feel when they are in the restaurant, what the vision we are trying to bring to life is, and why customers should choose this place to celebrate, come together, and spend their precious time at.

Lighting is very important in creating an ambience as well as harmony and synergy between all the elements of the project, in order to transport guests to a different place. Our designs are people-oriented in that we emphasise conviviality and enhance human connection.

**What is a typical day in the studio like?**

Client presentations, briefs, works-in-progress, and workshops with designers.

**People's tastes evolve with time. Are your creative concepts for restaurants and bars influenced by trends? Should they be a main consideration when it comes to branding?**

We do not respond to trends – rather, we create concepts relevant to location and culture, in that they offer a sense of place and a sense of culture.

**The F&B landscape in Hong Kong is an ever-evolving one where East often meets West, and old often meets new. Does this make it challenging to come up with new creative concepts all the time?**

Hong Kong has transformed drastically in the past 12 years, evolving from a trading platform to a cultural hub. The F&B scene has shifted from high-end hotel restaurants to F&B destinations forming their own neighbourhoods. Hong Kong has also evolved from a city where people look elsewhere for inspiration, to a city people look to for inspiration. The dynamic F&B landscape does not make it challenging for us, but rather, more exciting because it is constantly changing.

**What do you think has been the common denomination of success for A Work of Substance so far?**

Clients come to us looking for substance, defined as the most essential or most vital part of an idea or an experience. We define the DNA of each brand and use that to inform every detail of the design. The reason we chose the word 'substance' as our name is because it speaks to our purpose to inspire.

Undulating lines breathe life into Hokkaidon's visual identity and interiors to reflect the restaurant's fresh menu.
*page 032*

The Ocean's menu design embodies the restaurant's namesake through texture and colour.
*page 148*

Bibo's lively aesthetic fuses the authenticity of Art Deco and street art with the sophistication of refined French gastronomy.
*page 168*

"Visual identities are important because they translate the craft that happens in the kitchen and bar. The visual stimulation helps to complete a backdrop for experiences that people will remember and get inspired by."

The alluring interiors of Paradis bar transport creatures of the night to a different time and place.
*page 252*

### Why are effective visual identities important in a dining and drinking experience?

The best dining experiences are all-immersive and all-consuming, in that they are 'transportative' and engaging to all the senses. To achieve this, restaurateurs and designers must consider every detail, which includes the visual identity. The best visual identities help the restauranteur tell their story, build the connections and links between the interior and the food, and then tie them all together to make sense.

### What inspires your creative output?

All of our work is guided by five main principles: curiosity, consideration, concept, narrative, and collaboration. We question, explore, and discover. We don't like predictability, clichés, categories, or things being forced. We always aim to develop connections that aren't obvious at first, but soon seem like they were always meant to be. This means our inspiration is broad-reaching and diverse for every project. We read, and are all actively engaged in popular culture, art, and design. We enjoy a studio made up of an international team with different backgrounds, interests, and points of view. All of these things inspire and influence our output.

### How would you like customers to enjoy and experience your work?

Good design is empathetic, unpredictable, confident, and intuitive. This is what we strive for in all of our work. For us, the most alluring design always has a distinctive narrative, and a point of view that gives a twist on the predictable. It has aspects that charm and inspire; and it tells a specific visual story. We love that people often don't notice our work as graphic design and branding – that it blends into a space and creates an atmosphere and feeling that people can't necessarily pinpoint. It weaves throughout the experience seamlessly to create a cohesive and wholesome experience.

### Storytelling forms the heart of your studio's creative philosophy. How does this apply specifically to branding restaurants and bars?

Every aspect of a bar or restaurant's offering influences how to tell its story. Whether it is casual, beer-forward, loud, and lower-priced or more elevated, cocktail-forward, refined but approachable, each concept we work on has its own unique offering and perspective. The best way to entice the ideal customer is to ensure that its own story is clear, so that people have some understanding of what to expect. And if you can tell that story in a way that is charming, interesting, or even humorous, the more enticing it will be to potential customers. As such, we spend time meticulously crafting the detail and nuance while keeping an eye on the bigger picture to deliver a product that is interesting, relevant, and excites us along the way. We do believe that the quality of the concept and the operator's ability to execute the idea in the best way possible is extremely important. We want what we are selling to be genuine.

### With so many diverse projects under Glasfurd & Walker's belt, what is your creative process for restaurants and bars typically like?

Hospitality projects are unique in that they involve so many personal, visceral, and sensorial experiences for the customer. You have to consider many nuances such as cuisine style, price point, interior, ambience, service style, and the character of the place. You also have to imagine the customer journey from how they would first discover the concept to arriving, being seated, how the menus work and feel to finishing their meal and receiving the bill. This gives us more opportunities to be creative compared to many corporate or retail concepts. The touchpoints within a restaurant while the guest is there allows us a certain freedom to deviate from strict brand guidelines because the customer is in the space having their experience curated.

### How do you overcome challenging briefs?

The most challenging briefs for us are when a client doesn't have a point of view or embody the concept that they want to create. In these instances, we spend a lot of time helping to put them in touch with the right partners to help make the project a success, so that their dreams and business can be realised. For a project to be successful, every point of the experience – not just its branding – must be cohesive and thought through.

Citing curiosity, consideration, and collaboration as important foundations of their distinct creative approach, Canada-based Glasfurd & Walker are masters of storytelling when it comes to designing visual identities. With a striking portfolio that spans a variety of industries including F&B and hospitality, it combines concept and craft to deliver memorable experiences for patrons through eye-catching and effective work that leaves lasting impressions. BRANDLife delves into the studio's philosophy for branding restaurants and bars in the following interview with its co-founders, Phoebe Glasfurd and Aren Fieldwalker.

# Glasfurd & Walker

Dialogue with Co-founders
Phoebe Glasfurd & Aren Fieldwalker

"For us, the most alluring design always has a distinctive narrative and a point of view that gives a twist on the predictable. It has aspects that charm and inspire; and it tells a specific visual story."

(Top & left) Botanist's visual identity feature a stylish interpretation of the Pacific Northwest's lush earthiness.
*page 112*

The story and heritage of Earls 67
remains the focus of its updated
globalised visual identity.
**page 052**

**What is a typical day in the studio like?**

Each day, we start with creative meetings with
the team to discuss the previous day's work and
what's on for that day. Undoubtedly, poolside
chill playlists play indefinitely in the background
while our dog, Jersey, licks anyone entering…to
death. We set daily goals and milestones for each
team member to ensure our projects are on track
and delivered on time. Each day varies based on
stages of projects but we typically have a number
of client meetings and creative brainstorming
sessions for each department and team member.
One day a week, we have a full studio production
meeting covering all current and new projects,
any priority discussion points on any project, and
confirming what the current and next week's
workloads look like for the team.

**Could you share any branding or interior project
for a restaurant or bar that you were impressed
by lately and why?**

The Collectionist Hotel in Sydney is a great
example of interior work and collaboration
between multiple creatives. We particularly love
the custom carpets by designer Elke Kramer. A
great example of graphics being translated into an
interior environment.

**What is your dream project?**

Given the scope of work the studio has created
since inception, one of the remaining projects
the studio would love to be involved in is a luxury
boutique hotel project that includes a bar and/or
restaurant. From top to bottom. We'd also love to
design a fragrance brand, including the custom
packaging and glass.

The F&B scene in Russia today may be a highly competitive one, but DA. Design & Architecture are thriving in the midst of it. Although young, the bureau has been involved in various design projects that stand out with their modern minimalist aesthetic that combines a clever use of space and volume. Founded by four team members––of which three are architects––it places emphasis beyond form; championing functionality through organisation, materials, and details. The team's following interview with BRANDLife provides further insight into their creative philosophy, process, and aspirations,

# DA. Design & Architecture

Dialogue with Co-founders
Fedor Goreglyad, Boris Lvovskiy, Anna Lvovskaia
& Partner Maria Romanova

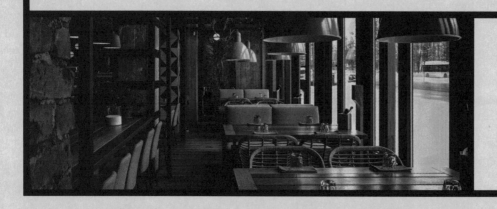

### Why are well-designed interiors important for a memorable dining and drinking experience?

We are convinced that good design gives a restaurant about 30% of its success. First of all, the design is responsible for the attractiveness of the place, so that a person passing by would stop and say, 'Wow! I want to visit it!'. Thus, the interior forms the first impression that a visitor would have and is an important element in giving a general idea of it – the concept of the kitchen and so on. Certainly, a good interior isn't enough for a successful restaurant – service, food presentation, and quality are altogether of equal importance here. However, without an interesting design, nobody would want to visit this place.

### Space and volume seem to be a priority for your projects. How would you define a competently organised space for a restaurant or bar?

When working on a project, we always devote a lot of time and effort to planning and developing the concept and spatial solutions for the interior, as we consider them the basis that makes it possible to introduce almost any decorative solution. Space determines to what extent visitors will feel comfortable in a place, and what impression the interior creates; for example, whether it is more private or open, a bar or a restaurant, for long dinners or quick snack breaks. In addition, a properly organised space will allow staff to work comfortably and efficiently, which will also influence the overall impression of service.

### Would you ever move into the finer details like product design to complement your spatial work?

In all our projects, we try to work together and guide a team of graphic designers who develop the corporate identity, so that it is in harmony and complementary with the interior. We are not specialists in graphic design, and we believe it is more correct when it is developed by professionals. However, of course, the project looks 100% harmonious only when everything from the graphic elements and food presentation to the servers' uniforms is connected with the interior or in the same style.

### After so many projects over the years, how do you choose which projects or clients to work with?

We love it when we are approached by professionals in their field. Almost always, such people know what they want, and at the same time, understand the importance of the creative component, so they respect our work and are receptive to our ideas and opinions. As a result, projects with these clients turn out to be more interesting and harmonious.

### How have the F&B establishments and their interiors in Russia evolved over the years?

The restaurant market in St. Petersburg and in Russia as a whole is now experiencing rapid growth. A lot of companies are being opened, but at the same time, a lot of them are also closing down as there is a lot of competition. More and more people in Moscow and St. Petersburg are preferring to have lunch and dinner outside the house today, which is why the luxury restaurants of the early 2000s have made way for simple but fashionable and interesting places for the every day. As such the interiors of these places need to be spectacular, interesting and memorable, but created with a relatively small budget.

### Could you share any interior project that you were inspired by lately?

We visited Kiev recently and were impressed by a lot of the local projects. The interiors of Vietnamese kitchen-restaurant NAM, designed by YOD Design Lab, as well as concept hotel BURSA, designed by 2B.Group stood out to us the most.

# "...a properly organised space will allow staff to work comfortably and efficiently, which will also influence the overall impression of service."

(Top & right) PORT 2.0's interior concept represents a balanced mix of rough industrial chic and Scandinavian minimalism.
*page 222*

tom-made illumination featuring a fishing
-inspired design adds character to PORT
's space and references the marine theme.
222

(Top right & bottom) Restaurant Kompaniya's
warm wooden elements and green accents envelop
patrons in its cosy and friendly vibes.
*page 178*

**Why are well-designed interiors important for a memorable dining and drinking experience?**

Customers today are not just looking to eat good food, but to also enjoy a unique experience when entering a restaurant or bar. Where they would typically only focus on the quality of the menu before, more and more emphasis is being placed onto the design of the interior as well as the ambience it creates. A well-designed space results in fluid circulation overall; helping the whole dining or drinking experience become 'one'.

**What drives your creative output?**

First of all, our clients. Their history, philosophy, and knowledge of what they are going to offer are as important as the actual design elements. We design for humans and for this reason, they are our first input. We would also like customers to feel unique in every space we design. If we achieve this, we would have reached a point of uniqueness in our design that we can be satisfied about. Secondly, we get a lot of inspiration during our trips around the world, as well as from other creative disciplines like fashion and art.

**In a creative city like Valencia, do changing customer appetites ever affect your aesthetics?**

Trends have a big influence on our daily life in general, and customers are driven by trends made visible in a massive way through social media. For this reason, although we need to keep them in mind, we always strive to go further by focusing on the future and not just what is actually popular at the time. That said, we work with all kinds of brands, so every project is different and requires a unique approach. As such, trends aside, the main thing for us is to work with entrepreneurs who are passionate about what they do.

**Does your creative approach for restaurants and bars differ from the other non-hospitality brands you work with?**

Our approach for bars and restaurants starts from our personal passion to go out for dinner. We are people that like to enjoy a visit to a restaurant or bar. For us, it is important to do these visits not only to enjoy the experience personally, but to also learn from each type of restaurant/bar and look at how they are set up. This means that we not only get to study what we like, but also look at the type of restaurants that we usually do not visit so we can learn from every business model.

**Your portfolio includes stylish product design. Do you create the furniture or fittings for all of your interior projects, or have a favourite piece?**

We try to custom-make products for every project, especially for restaurants and bars. Under certain circumstances, typically for bigger hotel chains and offices, this is not always possible, so customisation takes up about 20% of the projects instead of 80% like the rest of the smaller ones. Out of all the products we have designed specifically for a brand, we probably like the Wink lamps we did with Houtique the most!

**After so many projects over the years, how do you choose projects or clients to work with?**

We are open to any project for honest and passionate people; whether it is a freelancer who wants to open a small 20sqm store or a corporate company that wants to open a big hotel. If they like what we do and feel comfortable with what we share with them during our first conversations together, then we would be more than happy to work with them!

# Masquespacio

Dialogue with Co-founders
Ana Milena Hernández Palacios & Christophe Penasse

One would be hard-pressed not to smile upon seeing the de-light-inducing design work by Masquespacio, an award-win-ning creative consultancy based in Spain. Featuring bright and charming colour combinations as well as thoughtful yet play-ful applications of shapes and lines, its distinctive spaces are as warm and welcoming for patrons as they are chic, charming, and wonderfully crafted. To find out more about the inspiration and principles that drive their projects forward, BRANDLife speaks to co-founders Ana Milena Hernández Palacios and Christophe Penasse for the following interview.

Kaikaya's colourful tiles and wooden accents brighten up the dining and drinking area.
*page 188*

(Top & left) Stepping into Hikari is akin to stumbling upon an authentic 'izakaya' tucked between a maze of Tokyo alleyways.
*page 200*

"[Our clients'] history, philosophy, and knowledge of what they are going to offer are as important as the actual design elements. We design for humans, and for this reason, they are our first input."

Kaikaya fuses Japanese influences with Brazilian tropicalismo in a compelling manner through structure and nature.
*page 188*

# Biography

## A Work of Substance

A Work of Substance was founded amidst Hong Kong's design revolution. The studio uses design as a tool to rejuvenate culture and local neighbourhoods, while creating works of substance that make the city a source of inspiration. Ever-daring and ever-curious, they constantly venture into new projects and industries through commissions that span the globe.

## Anagrama

Anagrama is an international branding, architecture, and software development firm with offices in Monterrey and Mexico City. They work towards the right balance between being a design boutique and a business consultancy for companies in various industries around the world. Their focus lies in developing creative pieces and paying the utmost attention to details, while providing the best solutions based on the analysis of tangible data.

## ater.architects

ater.architects is a Kyiv-based interior design studio that was founded by Alexander Ivasiv and Yuliya Tkachenko. The studio specialises in designing private and public interiors such as cafés, bars, restaurants, offices, and medical institutions, as well as furniture and lighting pieces to realise their concepts.

## BUCK.STUDIO

BUCK.STUDIO is a Wroclaw-based, multidisciplinary design and consultancy office specialising in the food and beverage, hospitality, and retail sectors. With international recognition and design awards under their belt, they believe that the best ideas always come from teamwork, where courage, creativity, and consistency are equally as important as an open mind, insightful observation, and a sense of humour. The team consists of both young and versatile designers as well as experienced technical designers and professionals.

## Chapter

Chapter is a Monterrey-based design studio that focuses on the core work involved in creating a brand; trusting that design as the end result will be beautiful, coherent, and timeless. The team believes that strategy and personality are key components that need to exist within each brand behaviour and application for clients to thrive.

## DA. Design & Architecture

DA. Design & Architecture is a Saint Petersburg-based architecture bureau that specialises in the food and beverage sector. Although its team is young, it has already won several prestigious awards in the field of design, such as the Grand Prix of the ADD Awards. Their modern minimalist style and creative approach to space regularly land their projects in local and international publications and media.

## Dutchscot

Dutchscot in London combines knowledge, beauty, and audacity to create original, long-lasting, and meaningful work that lives happily through any of the usual – and unusual – disciplines. The team is driven by both intuition and collective experience from working at some of the most renowned design and branding agencies today. Besides collaborations, it also believes in creating engaging relationships that go the distance.

## El Equipo Creativo

El Equipo Creativo is an interior design and architecture studio based in Barcelona. As design specialists of gastronomic, commercial, and hospitality spaces since 2010, they have worked with Michelin-starred restaurants and some of the most prestigious chefs in the world, such as Ferran Adrià. Winner of American Architecture Prize's Firm of the Year 2017 and more than 20 international awards, their projects have been recognised worldwide in the general press as well as publications about trends and design like FRAME, which selected them as one of the 20 most influential designers in the world.

## Foreign Policy Design Group

Foreign Policy Design Group are a team of idea makers and storytellers who help clients and brands realise and evolve through the creative and strategic use of traditional and digital media channels in Singapore. Helmed by creative directors Yah-Leng Yu and Arthur Chin, they work on a wide variety of projects spanning creative and art direction, design, branding, research, strategy, and marketing campaign services for luxury fashion and lifestyle brands, fast-moving consumer goods brands, arts and cultural institutions as well as think tank consultancies.

pp 028-031

## Glasfurd & Walker

Glasfurd & Walker provide strategic design services that focus on brand creation, development, and management. The studio creates strong brand stories, narratives, and creative work that are thoughtful, strategic, and genuine yet surprising, engaging, beautiful, and memorable.

pp 052-055, 112-117, 262-265

## Here Design

Here Design is a London-based design studio that specialises in crafting beautiful, useful, and authentic cultural objects and experiences. Founded in 2005 by partners Caz Hildebrand, Mark Paton, and Kate Marlow, the team work across a wide range of projects backed by the firm belief that it makes them better designers. Whether they are designing a book, bottle packaging, or an exhibition, their intention is always to create rich, engaging visual worlds that bring brands to life in three dimensions.

pp 040-043

## HOUTH

HOUTH is a creative studio based in Taiwan that flexibly integrates creativity, strategy, design, and resources to create fresh narratives and solutions for clients.

pp 036-039

## Ideando

Ideando is a design studio that integrates innovation and execution. It provides design and consulting services for clients in the commercial and cultural sectors by understanding contexts, defining concepts, striving for accuracy and clarity, as well as building relationships and experiences.

pp 082-085, 098-101

## Jaeho Shin

Jaeho Shin is a graphic designer who was born in 1993. Currently based in South Korea, he is working as part of the graphic design and art direction team, Unofficial (Uofc.)

pp 126-129

## LIE DESIGN & ART DIRECTION

LIE stands for Little Ideas Everyday, an independent graphic design studio based in Kuala Lumpur. Founded in 2011, LIE works across a diverse range of visual communication projects; constantly seeking fresh approaches to provide beautiful and innovative solutions for clients, as well as self-initiated projects. Instead of sticking with the norm or established patterns, it believes that there is always room to explore in design.

pp 064-067

## LMNOP

LMNOP in New York specialises in creating unique identities with a playful edge. Infusing style and energy into businesses of all sorts, the studio helps to bring a company's ideas and inspiration to life. Having carved a niche for itself in the hospitality sector to include branding for restaurants and bars, food and beverage packaging, as well as hotel and travel concept ideation, it recognises the power of a well-crafted brand in ensuring success. While the team do not take themselves too seriously, they are serious about the work they do – believing that the best work is done on a full stomach.

pp 044-047

## Madison Tierney

Madison Tierney is a Melbourne-based graphic designer who specialises in creative design, strategy, and art direction, while dabbling in words. She is particularly seduced by publications, identities, and typography.

pp 130-133

## Masquespacio

Masquespacio is an award-winning creative consultancy that was created in 2010 by Ana Milena Hernández Palacios and Christophe Penasse. Combining its founders' two disciplines – interior design and marketing – the Spanish design agency specialises in interior and branding projects through a unique approach that results in fresh and innovative concepts that continue to gain international recognition. Their client list extends across countries worldwide, including Norway, the USA, France, Portugal, Germany, and Spain.

pp 188-193, 200-203, 270-273

## Mildred & Duck

Mildred & Duck is a Melbourne-based graphic design and communication studio established by Sigiriya Brown and Daniel Smith. It designs for print, digital, and environmental media to create solutions that communicate and connect with people. Working across a variety of sectors with a range of clients including start-ups and established organisations, Mildred & Duck deliver thoughtfully crafted and thoroughly-executed outcomes regardless of scope or budget.

pp 056-059

## Minas Kosmidis

Minas Kosmidis or Architecture in Concept in Thessaloniki was established in 2007, and undertakes local and international architecture and interior design projects. Over the years, the studio has created a diverse portfolio in the fields of private housing, hospitality, and retail; focusing on the food service and entertainment sectors. Many of its projects have been featured in renowned magazines and international competitions.

pp 228-233

## moodley brand identity

moodley brand identity is an international award-winning strategic design agency that has been developing corporate and commercial brands since 1999. Whether it is for a start-up, market launch, or repositioning project, the studio sees its creative responsibility in the strategic development of simple, intelligent, and emotionally appealing solutions to complex tasks in meeting the modern demands of digital transformation.

pp 060-063

## NC Design & Architecture Ltd

NC Design & Architecture Ltd (NCDA) is a Hong Kong-based architectural design firm specialising in residential, commercial, and hospitality projects. It seeks to develop creative work that reinvents the experience of space through meaningful connections. Using storytelling as its basis of inspiration, the studio's projects exist at the intersection of art and architecture and help start creative collaborations, stimulate interesting conversations, and deliver projects that tell a unique story.

pp 216-221, 234-239

## Outline

Outline is a global creative company focused on branding and brand narratives, website design and development, as well as brand experiences. It challenges clients to abandon pretense, embrace authenticity, and be themselves by using art and language to help them be seen in new ways, be understood more deeply, and be actively engaged with their audiences. The team obsess over details, fight for good ideas, and get things done on time from their base in South Carolina.

pp 118-121

## Perky Bros

Perky Bros was established in 2009 to help brands gain clarity, value, and distinction through design. The Nashville-based studio creates visual identities, websites, packaging, print materials, and any odds or ends necessary to create an authentic experience. From start-ups to more established brands, it keeps its approach flexible and strives to offer solutions built on plain-spoken, ambitious ideas — always grounded in research and meticulous craft.

pp 048-051

## Post Projects

Post Projects is a graphic design and consulting studio in Vancouver. Driven to evolve their craft and honour the legacy of contemporary design, they work with a wide range of clients that share their belief in design's ability to tell a story, stir an emotional response, and communicate with a clarity that is more than the sum of its parts. Through a rigorous process backed by meticulous research, the studio strives to create work that surprises, delights, and stands the test of time.

pp 078-081

## Rabih Geha Architects

Rabih Geha Architects is a team of architects and designers working together to create spaces that inspire. Led by Rabih Geha, the award-winning practice works on a portfolio of projects that include architecture, interiors, product design, and experimental installations. Representing a young generation of architects bucking tradition in favour of a new approach, it works alongside its clients to weave together the story of both their identities and the buildings they inhabit. Based in the creative heart of Lebanon, the practice was founded in 2006 and Geha's authenticity remains at the forefront. Each project retains an individual identity based on the stories it has to tell.

pp 164-167

## Re

Re believes that to stay relevant, brands need to behave like living, breathing entities that constantly evolve with the world around them. With David Bowie as their muse, the studio team build brands by giving them the innate ability to adapt in response to moments in time, all while remaining unmistakably themselves. Inspired by the meaning of the studio name, which means 'again and again' in Latin, they use a process of ongoing iteration to enable brands to adapt as new business and cultural opportunities present themselves; working from offices in Sydney, London, Greater China, and Los Angeles.

pp 068-071

## Savvy Studio

Savvy is a design, architecture, and branding studio based in New York and Mexico. Working across the globe, it is focused on sharing unique stories and creating exceptional concepts that endure over time.

pp 138-141

## SDCO Partners

SDCO Partners is a multi-disciplinary studio of designers, developers and thinkers based in Charleston. The team is made up of listeners and storytellers who combine imaginative ideas with thoughtful design solutions to craft and cultivate brands.

pp 102-107

## Sella Concept

Sella Concept is a non-conventional design studio and business consultancy based in London. Its philosophy is to re-invent the retail, hospitality, and corporate industry by creating site specific brands. Excited by design and inspired by consumer experiences, the team believe that a unique offering drives a culture and long-lasting patron base to help visionary clients realise the true value of their real estate and business.

pp 144-147

## Spacemen

Spacemen was founded in early 2014 by Edward Tan and Kyan Foo as a design firm that specialises in building brand architecture. Storytellers of space through architecture and interiors, it transforms primary brand strategies and ideologies into one-of-a-kind spatial experiences from its base in Shanghai.

pp 204-209

## Studio Band

Studio Band takes a brutal approach to design, in that what it does is shaped by what it does not do. Without settling for anything 'not quite right', over-designed, or under-designed, it offers creative and effective solutions by thoroughly understanding the task at hand from its base in Adelaide. The studio favours form and function over flourish and fads, taking each brief as an opportunity to further refine its craft. Besides placing as much value in the process as the finished piece, it considers insight its most powerful tool in achieving honest and timeless design.

pp 122-125

## Studio Frisch

Krists Darzins is the independent designer behind Studio Frisch, with vast experience in designing and branding products and services for businesses of various kinds. Currently working with international clients on creative digital solutions and mindful visual identities from his base in Riga, his work style is all about creating the best solution for every need. To achieve success in design, he believes in going deep into the brand's core, rather than merely skimming the surface.

pp 108-111

## The Colour Club

The Colour Club is a Sydney-based creative studio that works across a variety of disciplines to help brands gain genuine desirability and distinction through design. Strategic thinking, a collaborative approach, and a love of the craft allow the team to cultivate tailored solutions for clients of all sizes.

pp 134-137

## The Lab Saigon

The Lab is a creative studio in Ho Chi Minh City that tip-toes along the intersections of branding, interior design, web design, communication, film production, and other disciplines.

pp 086-089

## Thinking*Room

Thinking*Room is a design company based in Jakarta. Founded in 2005 and known for pushing the limits, it focuses on conceptual solutions; providing full design services including brand identities, strategy, campaigns, content creation, product and packaging design, books, websites, social media, motion, interiors, and installations.

pp 090-093, 094-097

## WEIJENBERG

WEIJENBERG is a multidisciplinary studio based in Singapore. It is made up of dynamic team members driven by the ambition to push boundaries and move boldly – likening themselves to 'dreamers and doers who are happiest when unthinking convention and tailoring design to the physical world'. Led by the next generation and inspired by local values and conditions, theyfirmly believes in honest architecture and a healthy environment.

pp 246-251

## Xiamen Fancy Design & Decoration Co., Ltd.

Xiamen Fancy Design & Decoration is an award-winning architecture firm founded by Fang Guoxi. Its creative philosophy revolves around the concept that 'a touching piece of design starts from life and expresses itself through beauty'; as exemplified by its projects in the F&B industry.

pp 240-245

## YøDezeen Architects

YøDezeen is an award-winning architectural and interior design studio operating worldwide from their base in Kiev and specialising in a variety of contemporary styles. Established in 2011 by architects and fellow students Artem Zverev and Artur Sharf, the studio offers a custom multidisciplinary approach to high-end design. YøDezeen has extensive international experience in both residential and commercial projects, using their professional philosophy to create customised aesthetic solutions for clients by mixing timeless designs with striking architecture.

pp 154-159

## Acknowledgements

We would like to specially thank all the designers and studios who are featured in this book for their significant contribution towards its compilation. We would also like to express our deepest gratitude to our producers for their invaluable advice and assistance throughout this project, as well as the many professionals in the creative industry who were generous with their insights, feedback, and time. To those whose input was not specifically credited or mentioned here, we truly appreciate your support.

## Future Editions

If you wish to participate in viction:ary's future projects and publications, please send your portfolio to:
submit@victionary.com